MEN AND MONUMENTS

ON THE EAST AFRICAN COAST

1. Fort Jesus, Mombasa.

MEN AND MONUMENTS
ON THE EAST AFRICAN
COAST

by

JAMES S. KIRKMAN

FREDERICK A. PRAEGER, *Publishers*
New York · Washington

BOOKS THAT MATTER

Published in the United States of America in 1966
by Frederick A. Praeger, Inc., Publishers
111 Fourth Avenue, New York 3, N.Y.

Copyright © 1964, James S. Kirkman, London, England
Library of Congress Catalog Card Number: 66-18745

Printed in Great Britain

Contents

List of Illustrations

Figures

Foreword

by

Sir Mortimer Wheeler

EMBATTLED IN his Fort Jesus at Mombasa, Mr James Kirkman is in as fine a position as were his Portuguese predecessors to survey the African East Coast, with Kenya of course in the foreground. When I first knew the Fort it was still a thriving gaol, full of the picturesque unfortunates of the locality and looking not unlike what it must have looked almost any time this three-and-a-half centuries and more. Today it is a National Monument, containing a trim museum and the hospitable Maison Kirkman, and its visitors are volunteers. If in the process of transmutation it has inevitably acquired something of that air of unreality and desiccation which is the penalty of monumental immortality, the price was well worth the paying. The old castle, which must be the finest of its kind, has had a stormy life and may now be allowed to rest. We are reminded that it has changed hands nine times, and that in its greatest siege, that of 1696–8, upwards of four hundred Portuguese and several hundreds of Swahili died in its defence. It is pleasant to reflect that, yet again in its defence, Mr Kirkman and the Trustees of the Royal National Parks of Kenya have met a less exacting fate. In a changing world may their watchful beneficence long continue.

But if Mr Kirkman were confronted with the choice of a territorial title, he might well hesitate. Fort Jesus would be the more dramatic alternative; on the other hand I suspect that Gedi might win the day. In the years following 1948 he devoted skill and almost infinite labour to the recovery of this medieval Arab town and palace, sixty-five miles north of Mombasa, from the dense bush which had almost hidden it. The result was, and is, the display of a wide range of colonial Arab architecture such as had not previously been accessible anywhere along the East Coast. More than that, for the first time the potential value of the historical archaeology of this semi-alien region was demonstrated. In time to come, our successors will look back to Gedi as the first systematic attempt to open up a phase of the African past which extends over-all from Roman times through Arab, Persian, Indian, Chinese, and European contacts down to that colonial era which is already cooling in the mould of history. And behind and amidst all this is the reaction of a varied and shifting assemblage of older African peoples, who looked uneasily upon the confused, kaleidoscopic scene—and waited.

In his present book Mr Kirkman travels in but also far beyond his own Kenya, and we are his debtors for doing so. The history and archaeology of the East African coast have been a unitary problem, and may be so again. In recent years a British Institute of History and Archaeology has been established in East Africa and has already been busy in the south, in Tanganyika, upon collateral sites. If during the next ten years exploration and excavation, hand in hand with documentary research, proceed as they have lately been proceeding both on the coast and in the interior—and there is still ample room for acceleration—the traditional Darkness of Africa will be as much an anachronism as the Dark Ages of Britain and Greece and India are rapidly becoming. And for the same reason: the advent of trained minds and hard work.

London, 1964   MORTIMER WHEELER

Preface

THE OBJECT of a preface is to tell the reader what he is going to get and to attempt to mollify the critic by explaining why he doesn't find what he expects, all in the shortest number of words.

I have tried to tell the story of the coast of East Africa through its monuments in a way that will appeal to the general public. There are two main difficulties in carrying out this purpose; first, there has been comparatively little work done on the subject; secondly, the austere nature of the material has little of the ready appeal of the monuments of Europe and Asia.

As an archaeologist who has been working in Kenya for sixteen years, I am a primary source for the monuments of Kenya and I have a fair knowledge of the monuments of Pemba, Zanzibar and Tanganyika. I have also visited Mogadishu, Merca, Moçambique and Lourenço Marques. For most of Somalia and Madagascar I am dependent on others.

I have used the term "historical monuments" in its narrow sense, which excludes the prehistoric sites such as Olorgesaillie and the cave paintings of Tanganyika, and in fact limits the scope of the book to the coastal strip. There is one site, Engaruka in the Serengetti area, not far from Moshi, which I concede might have been included. However, Engaruka which is a collection of dry-stone structures, similar to the sites in Inyanga in Tanganyika, has not been excavated and has no similarities with any other sites in East Africa. Anything I could have said would have had very little value. I regret that the true African plays such a small part in this book, but the post-prehistoric Africans who lived in this area did not build historical monuments in the sense in which I have used the term.

I should like to express my great appreciation of the work of my colleague Neville Chittick in Tanganyika and of the historical researches of Mr. E. Axelson, Dr. Carlos de Azevedo, Professor C. R. Boxer, Mr. A. T. Curle, Dr. E. Cerulli, M. H. Deschamps, Sir John Gray, Dr. G. S. P. Freeman-Grenville, Dr. V. L. Grottanelli, Senhor A. Lobato and Dr. A. J. S. Prins. Finally I must thank my Director Mervyn Cowie, C.B.E., Dr. L. S. B. Leakey and the Trustees of the Royal National Parks of Kenya, who added archaeology to their many other burdens, and the Gulbenkian Foundation whose generous grant made possible the excavation and restoration of Fort Jesus. Archaeological research on the coast of East Africa only began in 1948, when the Trustees of the Royal National Parks of Kenya decided to foster this long neglected child whom nobody else would look at. Nine years later a Government Department of Archaeology was established in Tanganyika and after another two years the British Institute of History and Archaeology in East Africa was brought into being by the efforts of my old master Sir Mortimer Wheeler, K.B.E. Since this book was written there have been many changes in East Africa. The Royal National Parks of Kenya are now the Kenya National Parks. The District Commissioners, District Officers and Mudirs are now Regional Government agents. Zanzibar is no longer a Sultanate but part of the United Republic of Tanganyika and Zanzibar. The Past which was once a Future and before that a Present remains to mock and entertain us.

Mombasa,   JAMES S. KIRKMAN.
Kenya.

I

The Coast of East Africa

THE AREA covered by this book is the coastal belt which
extends from the Straits of Bab el Mandeb in the north to the
Limpopo in the south, and includes the islands of Pemba,
Zanzibar, the Comoros and Madagascar. All this enormous
stretch of coast, comprising two-thirds of the eastern side of
Africa, has been in direct contact with the southern shores
of Arabia, southern Persia, western India and the islands of
the Indonesian archipelago for over two thousand years.
This is the territory of Erythrean Africa, to borrow the
classical name taken from the *Periplus*. The *Periplus*, written
by an Alexandrian Greek in the reign of the Emperor Nero,
is a Route Book or "Pilot" of the Indian Ocean giving factual
information for traders, and as such is one of the few objective
books that have been written on this region. It is remarkable
in many ways, not least in that it is written by a professional
who had no need and no inclination to rely on the views of
colleagues or informants of doubtful veracity. He was also
under no obligation to make his book conform to any accepted
ideas on cosmography or politics. Anyone who reads the
Periplus will appreciate how much it differs from most of the
other literature on East Africa. The very early date of these
Asian contacts, perhaps the first millennium B.C., is to be
inferred from the spread of cultivated plants from the East
to Africa and from Africa to the East. There is so far no supporting archaeological evidence, but it need not necessarily
be denied. Primitive people have very few belongings and

15

some of them have even been able to dispense with pottery—the staple, often miserable diet of the field archaeologist. However, over large stretches of this coast there are no structural remains and there have been no excavations to find what relics of the past exist in the way of implements, ornaments and utensils.

From the beginning of the first millennium of the Christian era there are references to markets and even settlements, but so far nothing has been found to give historical references unquestionable archaeological body. A group of Roman and Seljuk coins was found at Burkao in Somalia but only reached the British Museum fifteen years later. The finder, who was educated and even literary, wrote an article on his experiences but never mentioned the coins. A similar group of coins is in the Zanzibar Museum enclosed in an envelope labelled with the name of a village in Pemba, but no details have been recorded. A coin of Ptolemy X is said to have been found near Dar-es-Salaam and lately a large red *millefiori* bead, which is probably Frankish, was picked up in a mangrove swamp at Kisiju, fifty miles south of Dar-es-Salaam. Nothing has been excavated to suggest a site of pre-Arab or even early Islamic date. The Indonesian period on the coast of East Africa has left no traces which have yet been identified, other than the speech of some of the tribes of Madagascar, the canoe with the double outrigger, some musical instruments, and perhaps the pillar tombs. The earliest fact to be found in East Africa between the Straits of Bab el Mandeb and Madagascar or between the Straits and Morocco, is the inscription in the tin-roofed mosque of Kizimkazi in Zanzibar dated 500 Hejira or A.D. 1107, and this was reset when the mosque was rebuilt in the eighteenth century. The Palace known as Husuni Kubwa and the adjacent building Husuni Ndogo at Kilwa, now being excavated by Neville Chittick, and are probably twelfth century.

The date and location of the first Islamic settlements has still to be established. The earliest imported ware which has been found is an earthenware with a green and yellow glaze and formal floral or random linear patterns, scratched through the paint under the glaze (see Plate 2). This ware could be as early as the tenth or eleventh century, which is the traditional date of the foundation of the first settlements in East Africa. It was found at Bhambor, the old Dabul (Pakistan) and Tîz (Persia), two old Indian Ocean ports, which flourished in the tenth and eleventh centuries and were alive in the thirteenth century. Sir Aurel Stein found sherds and wasters at Tîz and some of these appear to be identical with sherds found at Kilepwa, Gedi, Ras Makobe (Dar-es-Salaam) and other sites. They have also been found in Kenya with the sea-green celadon, which cannot be earlier than the thirteenth century and most of which is certainly fourteenth century, or later. The whole problem is an excellent demonstration of the necessity of determining not only when a thing was first made but when it was last made. This is extremely difficult, particularly in the East where traditional designs persisted far longer than in the western or classical worlds.

The long coast line is divided into two zones. From the Straits of Bab el Mandeb to Kisimayo it appears to consist of sandy wastes and scorched crags; further south there is a dry savanna, which extends to the Limpopo without obvious change. The savanna varies in cultivatability, largely due to the existence or non-existence of water and local variations of rainfall. Where conditions are favourable there are stretches of mangrove, and in the extreme south in the Zambezi basin tropical rain forest. Areas, invariably small, of rich agricultural potentiality occur rarely, notably on the west side of Pemba.

The terms "sandy wastes" and "dry savanna" must not be taken to mean that no agriculture was practised in one or that there were not dense patches of scrub in the other. The valley of the Webbe Shebeli has been cultivated for a thousand years but the way of living in Somalia has been overwhelmingly pastoral. The habits, ethics and politics of the nomad, with his eternal desire for fresh grazing for his herds, has governed the whole history of Somalia. The prosperity of the coastal cities depended on the preponderance of one tribe over the others, or a balance of power in which the possibility of victory was nicely balanced by the thought of the utter destruction which defeat would entail. Only when these conditions prevailed was there the peace and prosperity by which the products of the interior could reach the coastal cities.

In the "dry savanna" country a mixed economy was practised by small groups who were normally stationary. In the south on the Zambezi there were monarchial states, such as the Monomotapa of Zimbabwe, but political organization was not a necessity to the Bantu farmers, and they were frequently wise enough to do without it. Along the coast there is little evidence of it, except the shadowy King of the Zenj at Mombasa referred to by Idrisi, the semi-immigrant Kingdom of Shungwaya, and perhaps the Mutamandalin at Kilwa. The fact, however, that the Kilwans undertook expeditions against the "infidels" suggests that there were no states with whom they could deal in slaves to their mutual advantage. This happy state of anarchy was assisted by the patches of thick bush which hindered communications. The prosperity of the coastal cities in this area was derived from the gold that came from up country, the slaves that would normally come in the course of wars, and the ivory that was always available for those who had skill and courage to take it.

The attraction of East Africa was in the curiosities and rarities which she could provide, sometimes from the interior into which the foreign trader never ventured and for which he was dependent on intermediaries. These consisted of gold, copper, slaves, gums, ivory, leopard skins, tortoise-shell and rhinoceros horn. None was obtainable only in Africa, but all could be obtained in larger quantities and, ignoring the risk of total loss, at a greater profit from Africa than anywhere else. A prosperous voyage to Africa could set a man up for life, and the capital investment was not beyond the means of a merchant of even middle rank. The story of Sindbad the Sailor with its circumstantial impossibilities has all the verity of hopes and aspirations that were in some cases fulfilled. It is unfortunate that none of these success stories has been recorded, but there were certainly merchant princes in Cairo and Basra who made and enjoyed their gains from the East African trade until they were taken off them by an envious governor or sultan.

This is the background. The persons who concern us, however, are not those who went home but their not-so-prosperous relatives who stayed abroad, built their homes on the African coast, raised multicoloured families and founded the first colonial towns: Mogadishu, Barawa, Lamu, Pate, Malindi, Mombasa, Kanbalu (wherever it is), Kilwa, Sofala, old Zanzibar, and many small settlements. These grew up, decayed and were refounded wherever there was a chance of making a profit on an inhospitable and unpredictable coast. There are traditions of the foundation of many of these towns by settlers from the famous cities of the Islamic world and the stories, like the story of Sindbad, are basically true. On the other hand, they are family sagas in which most of the details between the departure from home and the time of the narrator have been forgotten. For example, a hypothetical Ali bin Muhammed came from Kufa. His descendant, a well-to-do merchant of Malindi, knows nothing of what happened when the family fell on hard times, wandered off to Sofala, went across the sea to Calicut and spent some generations in the Maldives before coming back to East Africa.

Then there were the exiles and the fugitives who left their country for the country's good, or as a result of political or religious disagreements; the gentry and the scholars who could not make money and were not very fond of hard work, but who introduced the elements of good living when they married into the merchant families; the craftsman and the artisans, the Benevenuto Cellinis, who left the centres of civilization when they got into hot water or found the competition too intense. The thirteenth century was a period of great misery in the eastern part of the Islamic world and the western, less disturbed countries could not take all the displaced makers of good things. Without these classes the coast would have remained a land of mud or grass huts like most of tropical Africa.

19

Most of these stories are stories of individuals, like the whole wicked history of colonialism, but as Dr. Prins has pointed out, there are a few examples of organized migrations. The most notable are the Almozaid, the Shirazi of Kilwa, the brothers Suleiman and Said of Lamu, and perhaps the Nabahani of Pate. These groups arrived with the intention of forming their own polities. The Almozaid disappeared, the Shirazi and the Nabahani founded the best integrated states of the coast.

Over all there was the spirit of Islam, the great faith in which the beggar has the respect and self-confidence of a king. In the present versatile world of infinite sources of inspiration, interest and consolation, where man in his loneliness can take comfort from the study of butterflies, stamps or obscure questions of the past, we forget the ages when the only escape or consolation was in the great religions.

To what standards of civilization the first settlements on the coast aspired, we have no knowledge. They were probably pioneer in the lowest sense of the word for a long time. The fact that the merchants of Mocha came from a town of luxury does not necessarily mean that they did anything about comfort and luxury in Africa. Many highly educated Europeans from London, Paris, Rome and even Boston, have lived in the most appalling squalor or austerity when they went abroad. A reading of history gives no support for any theory of consistency or inevitability, except perhaps the dismal law of diminishing returns. What could and should have happened is not necessarily what did happen.

The original population of the coast consisted of Bushman types whose implements have been found all over East Africa. In the next period, perhaps the middle of the first Christian millennium, the Bantu arrived on the coast. How, when and where we do not know. One view is that they reached the coast in the south, and then moved north up the coastal plain. Another is that they reached the coast in the north, following the course of the rivers. Both may be right. Their furthest northern settlements were on the Webbe Shebeli near Mogadishu.

20

2. Sherds of Islamic glazed ware from Gedi. *Top row:* Yellow and green *sgraffiato*, made in Persia or Iraq. From thirteenth-century levels. *2nd row:* Nos. 1 and 2. Yellow and black painted ware, perhaps made in the Hadhramaut. From fourteenth-century levels. No. 3. Chocolate and cream Champlevê ware, made in Persia. From fourteenth-century levels. *3rd and 4th row:* Blue-and-white painted wares of Kashan type, made in Persia. From fourteenth-century levels.

3(a) Plate with design of half acanthus leaves in manganese, blue and green on cream ground. Persian, from Gedi. Fifteenth or sixteenth century.

(b) Lid of jar in olive green celadon from Gedi. Fifteenth century.

The Bantu never penetrated the dry plains and mountains of northern Somalia; the original population was here replaced by the Somali and the Galla. None of these could be "the tall people of piratical habits" described in the *Periplus*. The Somali, originally on the coast of the Gulf of Aden, accepted both Islam and the Arabs who brought it to them. They drove the Galla westwards and southwards and became trading associates of the Arab towns of the Benadir—Mogadishu, Merca and Barawa. By the end of the fifteenth century the Somali were the dominant partners.

Three other tribal groups need to be mentioned to complete the picture of the human background of the historical monuments of East Africa. These are the Sanya, the Bajun and the Malagasy.

The Sanya, Ata or Boni are the hunting people of the coast, almost all of whom speak a form of Galla. Some, notably the Da'alo of the Lamu area, may be the remnants of the original Bushmanoid population, others are probably servile castes belonging to the Galla and Somali.

The Bajun are a fishing people living on the islands off the coast, from Kisimayo in Somalia to Pate in Kenya. At one time they also lived on the mainland, but were driven off it by the Galla. They may in part be descended from the Baduis of Barros, who were the Almozaid, followers of Zaid, the grandson of Hussein, who fled to Africa and founded the first settlements. Subsequently they were driven from their homes by successive waves of Arabs and became Africanized. Today all their clans except one have Somali eponyms, but they speak a form of Swahili very close to Giriama, a dialect of the north-east Bantu. Racially, they are extremely mixed but the Arab caste of face and temperament is usually unmistakable.

They are Muslim but rarely educated, and are generally looked down on by Arabs, Swahili, and Somali. They are probably less sanctimonious about alcohol and less suspicious of non-Muslims, but with regard to the various sexual frailties there is not much to choose between them. They work willingly and the loathsome tasks of cutting mangrove poles in the swamps, the drying of fish, and the cleaning of cowries are all done by the despised Bajun. They are fine boat builders, sailors, and occasionally silversmiths, but they apparently never acquired any skill in building, and make no claim to the mosques and tombs found on their islands. It is possible that they were the lower classes of the smaller coastal towns, who placed themselves under Somali patrons when the upper classes moved further south to what was then a quieter part of Africa. The first clear mention of them is at the end of the seventeenth century when they assisted the Portuguese in their attacks on Pate.

The Malagasy are derived from the Indonesian stock which peopled the Comoros and Madagascar. They consist of a large number of tribes, physically of mixed African and Indonesian stock but speaking a similar basically Indonesian tongue.

None of these peoples appear to have had any knowledge or interest in building, and the only historical monuments they seem to have left are the phallic grave stones which are ascribed to the Galla and the rather more schematized pillars of the Hova of Madagascar.

The Swahili language developed out of the speech of the north-east Bantu and became the home language of the mixed population of the coast, except in the north where Somali took its place. Both languages were strongly Arabized but they are African languages, and the coastal towns remained open through language to all the subconscious and immaterial influences that come through the spoken word.

The historical monuments of East Africa belong not to the Africans but to the Arabs and Arabized Persians, mixed in blood with the African but in culture utterly apart from the Africans who surrounded them. Certain Arab groups are more prominent than others, such as the Azdites and Nabahani, although at one time or other every Arab settlement must have contributed its quota, just as the population of America has been built up from all the old towns and villages of Europe. The absence of stone for building and the reluctance to use coral blocks has been a disability which accounts

for the modest nature of even the best buildings, such as the
Great Mosque at Kilwa (Plate 20a). The material was
generally coral rag and red earth or lime mortar. The mortar
and plaster that is made from the lime of burnt coral, if
properly prepared and matured, is superb. It is the only
reason why any of these buildings are standing, and the
resistance it has put up to the tremendous vegetation force of
the tropics is surprising. Some resemblance, based perhaps
largely on the material used, can be perceived between them
and the minor buildings of Persia. The Mbaraki Pillar at
Mombasa, which is a circular tower with a conical top built
in the seventeenth or early eighteenth century, is probably of
Persian inspiration (Plate 15). The *pishtaq* or monumental
gate in the wall of a court, as seen in the Palace at Gedi, is a
characteristic but not exclusive Persian architectural feature.
The standard house plan with the triple series of rooms and
the sunken court in front is borrowed from the Arab world.

In the fifteenth century there would seem to have been a
considerable development in trade with the East, and with
it an increase in Indian contacts. The curious pointed arch
without keystone or voussoirs, with the cut stones above the
apex giving an effect of an inverted Y, (Plate 13b) may be of
Indian inspiration. This arch is general along the stretch of
coast between Lamu and Tanga, although isolated examples
occur north and south of this area.

The scarcity of surviving monuments earlier than the
fifteenth century, the plainness of the architecture and the
simplicity of the ground plans, which never attained the
variety of complexity, make it difficult to trace a chain of
developments.

The most important buildings which have survived on
almost all sites are the Great Mosques or jumaa (Fig. 1a–f).
The oldest as we see them today are fifteenth century though
in some cases, as at Kilwa, older structures are incorporated
in them. Some of the other mosques, notably the Mosque of
Fakhr al Din at Mogadishu, are earlier. These were private
buildings whose continued existence was a matter for the
owner. Their construction was an act of piety, their main-

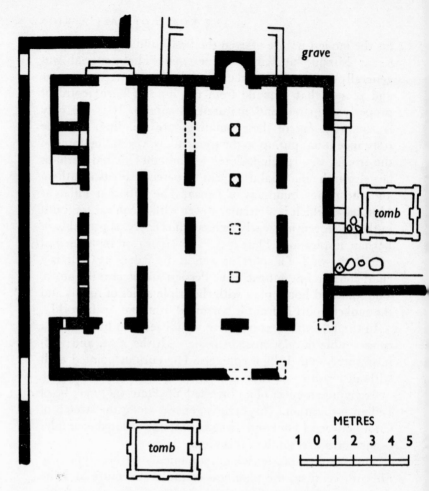

grave

tomb

tomb

METRES

1 0 1 2 3 4 5

FIG. 1a. *Plan of the mosque at Tongoni*

tenance had not the same merit, and in any case the family which built the mosque might die out or go away.

The form of roof construction also militated against a long life. It normally consisted of a lime concrete ceiling about twelve to fifteen inches thick, carried on square timbers, supported on square or octagonal pillars. So long as the timbers lasted, the roof held. When they began to decay, the roof sagged and pushed the walls out, unless it split and col-

24

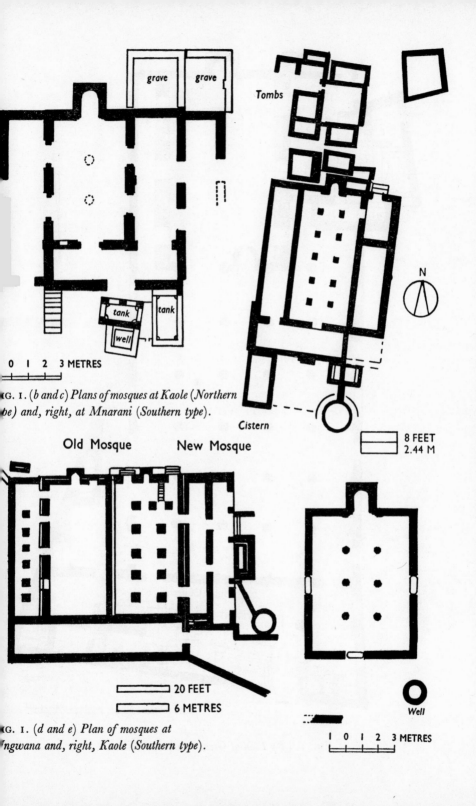

grave   grave

Tombs

tank   tank

well

N

0 1 2 3 METRES

FIG. I. (b and c) Plans of mosques at Kaole (Northern
type) and, right, at Mnarani (Southern type).

Cistern

8 FEET
2.44 M

Old Mosque   New Mosque

20 FEET

6 METRES

FIG. I. (d and e) Plan of mosques at
Ngwana and, right, Kaole (Southern type).

Well

1 0 1 2 3 METRES

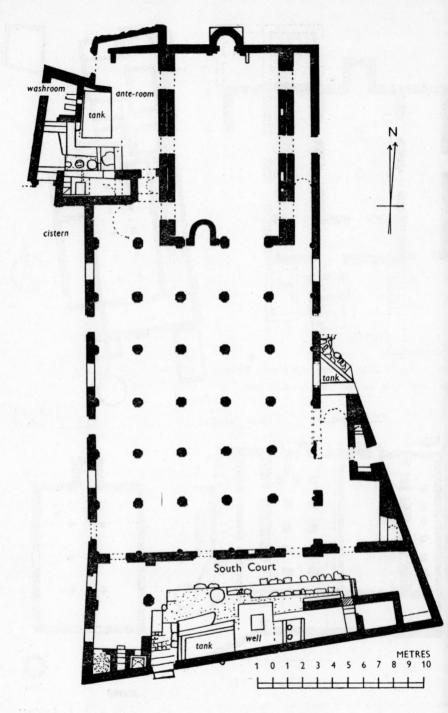

washroom

ante-room

tank

cistern

N

tank

METRES

1 0 1 2 3 4 5 6 7 8 9 10

South Court

tank

well

FIG. I. (f) *Plan of Great Mosque at Kilwa.*

lapsed inwards. This type of roof did not last much longer than a hundred or a hundred and fifty years. An alternative and better form of roof consisted of a series of small domes and barrel vaults. These were never as common as the flat roofs, and very few have survived. The finest example is the Great Mosque of Kilwa (Plate 20a). The only surviving example in Kenya is a small mosque at Mwana near Ungwana.

Neville Chittick has distinguished two types of mosque in Tanganyika: a northern provincial with aisles separated by walls, pierced with arches and a row of pillars down the centre; a southern, without aisles, with the roof carried on two rows of pillars, which were decently spaced, so as to leave an unobstructed view of the qibla. The distinction between mosques with a central row of pillars and those with two rows I agree is significant. Chittick's classification was intended to apply to Tanganyika only but is to some extent relevant to the whole coast. The northern type is certainly the commoner everywhere north of Kaole (Fig. 1b) but there exist many examples of the southern type, such as the Great Mosques at Ungwana (Fig. 1d), Luziwa (or Uziwa), Mnarani (Fig. 1c), and smaller mosques at Mogadishu (Fakhar al Din), Ungwana, Gedi and Mwana. Similarly the matter of aisles is significant, but outside Tanganyika it should not be associated with the pillars, which is a different problem. Mkumbuu, Shengeju and Shamiani, all on Pemba, have three rows of pillars but no aisles. It is possible that the addition of aisles is a practice which grew up in the fifteenth and sixteenth centuries.

Another distinction could be made between mosques with doors at the sides and those less common with a main door at the south end opposite the qibla, such as the Great Mosques of Mnarani and Kilwa (Fig. 1c, f). The ablution facilities were either outside, usually on the east side, or in the case of the second type at the south end, inside or outside the mosque. The remarkable second Great Mosque at Ungwana has two fine doorways, one on each side of the qibla, and the equally unusual Great Mosque of Mkumbuu a single door for the imam on the left side of the qibla. The pillar tombs, which

Chittick would prefer to call panel tombs because they are clearly a variety of a much larger group which had no pillars, are the only architectural peculiarity of East Africa. They will be discussed in their local setting. They may be related to the phallic pillars of the Konsu of southern Ethiopia. Murdock considers the Konsu to be a survival of a people he calls Megalithic Cushites, who had a highly developed system of irrigated agriculture and extended in small groups over most of East Africa. They were absorbed by the Bantu in the interior and by the Galla on the coast, but passed on to them a number of common cultural traits which these diverse peoples both possess. This theory is still purely conjecture and, even if true, does not explain how these pillars passed into Islamic culture. If the Megalithic Cushites were the inhabitants of the coast when the first Muslims arrived in the seventh century and accepted Islam *en masse*, one would have expected some tradition of their conversion to have survived.

The fifteenth century was the golden age of the Arab colonial culture of the coast. At the end of the century, the arrival of the Portuguese and the imposition of controls on trade in almost every commodity destroyed the basis on which these towns existed. The control was exercised capriciously and increasingly inefficiently, but it was sufficient to discourage the larger merchants on whose resources the various communities would depend for capital works, and to destroy the sense of security without which a community, apart from the individuals, cannot prosper.

During the next two centuries—the period of Portuguese domination—Mombasa, Kilwa and Pate, three of the major towns, and a number of places of less note such as Faza, Hoja (probably Ungwana) and the capital towns of Zanzibar and Pemba were destroyed with a varying proportion of their inhabitants. When the Portuguese were finally expelled at the end of the seventeenth century, the culture of the coast never revived. Victory had been achieved, not by the Arabs of the coast, but by their Omani cousins to whom the ultimate authority now devolved. The people themselves had changed, and conditions with them. The Galla had moved south, displacing the Bantu population that had lived more or less innocuously around the Arab mainland towns. These towns, now imperilled by a race of savage nomads, were evacuated, and in the course of the seventeenth century civilization came to an end over the mainland area between the semi-Somalized town of Mogadishu and Mombasa. Nothing as catastrophic occurred further south, although Kilwa never recovered from the destruction by the cannibals in 1586, and there is nothing to suggest any signs of prosperity before the development of the slave trade with the Europeans in the middle of the eighteenth century.

The islands of Lamu and Pate were outside the reach of the Galla and there, particularly at Lamu, the old life of the coast continued, although Pate, with its three towns of Pate, Faza and Siyu, received a large influx of immigrants from the mainland and lost its Arab character.

In the eighteenth century the two most important local authorities were the Nabahani sultans of Pate and the Omani governors of Mombasa, but the overlordship of the Sultan of Muscat, which he had earned by the expulsion of the Portuguese, was generally conceded by the Arabs of the towns between Mogadishu and Cape Delgado. North of Mogadishu he had no sovereign rights; the Comoros and Madagascar were similarly independent, while the Portuguese continued to govern the Kerimba Islands and the coastal settlements of Moçambique.

In the second quarter of the nineteenth century the interest taken by Seyyid Said, Sultan of Muscat, in his African dominions brought to an end the isolation which most of East Africa had enjoyed for about a hundred years. American, French, British and German merchants began to frequent the harbours of East Africa and were able to trade with reasonable security. They were very different from the Portuguese. They had no political or religious aspirations and were not unwelcome since their only interest was making money, an operation in which almost everybody made large profits.

Seyyid Said was an independent ruler but in one respect he had to defer to his British ally, who had saved him when threatened by his neighbours in Muscat and who protected him from other European powers in his African dominions. This was the embarrassing matter of the slave trade. The incomprehensible hostility of the British to one of the most respectable and lucrative of occupations, and the fanatical fury with which the British sailors attacked his subjects on the comparatively rare occasions when they were caught, was a pain to be endured, beside the unexampled prosperity of his dominions during his reign and the reigns of his successors.

In Madagascar a westernizing state came into existence with the unification of two-thirds of the island under the brilliant Hova King, Radama 1. Radama died prematurely in 1828, but the state he had created did not collapse. Madagascar, with its educational precociousness, its Protestant and Catholic French rivalries, and its oscillations between zenophobia and zenophilia, is reminiscent of both Uganda and Japan.

By the middle of the nineteenth century Africa had become a subject of intense interest to almost every restless mind of the age. The "Dark Continent" was penetrated from almost every side and for almost every conceivable motive. The explorers recorded what they saw irrespective of what it was, and published the results of their journeys when they returned to Europe. The nineteenth century was nothing if not an age of development. The discoveries of science seemed to show that every thing and every place could be put to some profitable use; Africa was not merely a land of wonders and horrors, but a land of potential wealth. Behind the explorers came the entrepreneurs with their pieces of paper which could be turned into concessions for themselves or treaties for their countries.

During the last two decades, Africa passed under European authority. For many years this was largely on paper, marked by different colours on the map, but eventually the whole area was brought under some code of law, though the remoter parts of Somaliland were not effectually controlled until after the First World War.

In the north, agreements between France and Britain gave to Britain most of the harbours on the Gulf of Aden and to France the Gulf of Tajura, where the terminus of the French railway to Addis Ababa was to be built. The remainder of Somaliland was given to Italy, together with the Benadir ports which had belonged to Zanzibar. The Sultanate of Zanzibar was reduced to the three islands of Zanzibar, Pemba and Mafia and was placed under British Protection. A stretch of ten miles deep on the mainland between the River Tana in the north and the River Umba in the south and the Lamu Archipelago were recognized as part of the Sultan's domains, but were united with the British Colony of Kenya for administrative purposes. The southern section of the mainland opposite Zanzibar, where in fact Zanzibar influence was greatest, between the River Umba and the boundary with Portuguese East Africa, had been taken by the new German Empire. After the First World War German East Africa became the Mandated Territory of Tanganyika which was administered by Britain until 1961. Beyond, considerably enlarged, was the colony of Portuguese East Africa. The Comoros and Madagascar were recognized as French Protectorates.

The European powers who ruled East Africa for fifty years have now withdrawn or are on the point of withdrawing. In the north the three Somalilands are reduced to two: the former British and Italian territories form the independent state of Somalia; French Somaliland has preferred to remain part of the French community. Of the component parts of the old Omani sphere, Tanganyika, Zanzibar, and Kenya have gained their independence. The three territories have a common language, race and history, and it is probable that they will eventually form a federal state so that the boundaries of Seyyid Said's commercial "empire" will one day be reconstituted.

In the far south, Madagascar is independent but the Comoros, like Djubuti, have preferred to remain inside the

French Community. Portuguese East Africa has been declared a part of Portugal.

The Portuguese domestic buildings and churches have disappeared. There remain only the magnificent fortresses, Jesus of Mombasa and S. Sebastião of Moçambique, and the padrão or cross brought by Vasco da Gama and erected at Malindi. There were never very many settlers north of the Zambezi and, from what is said of them, their standard of living was not high. It would be surprising if the houses in which they lived had survived.

The archaeological material proper is remarkably cosmopolitan. Pride of place is certainly held by the magnificent porcelain of China which stands out amongst the other jetsam of archaeology. Most of the sherds are from plates, bowls and jars; bottles, vases and flasks were never imported in numbers, and few specimens have been found. In the fourteenth and fifteenth century they were in sea-green ware known as celadon (Plate 2b) which was valued apart from its beauty and utility by the belief that it would reveal the presence of poison by cracking. As most well-to-do orientals expected to be poisoned at some stage of their life by a wife or son, it was prudent and reassuring to eat off celadon. It was perhaps embarrassing to notice a cracked plate at a feast but there is no advantage in life without a corresponding disadvantage. In the course of the fifteenth century blue-and-white porcelain became more and more popular although well into the seventeenth century there was a demand for celadon which was increasingly difficult to supply. Celadon is by no means common in sixteenth-century levels in East Africa and only a few sherds have been found in the seventeenth- and eighteenth-century levels in Fort Jesus, Mombasa.

Polychrome enamel porcelain was slow to reach East Africa but a fair number of pieces have been found in Fort Jesus, including late seventeenth- or early eighteenth-century *famille verte*. In the late eighteenth century small bowls and cups with festoons of miniature flowers and heavy borders in rose pink, aubergine, iron red, green and overglaze blue were imported in quantity. In the middle of the nineteenth

4. Door locks from inside houses at Lamu. Eighteenth or nineteenth century.
(a) Ebony inlaid with horn.
(b) Ebony decorated with silver.

5(a) Bronze horn or *siwa*, the horn of Lamu. Perhaps seventeenth century.

(b) Ivory horn or *siwa*, the horn of Pate, made at Pate 1680.

(c) Door in Zanzibar with characteristic carved ornament of Indian inspiration. Nineteenth century.

(d) Chair, ebony inlaid with ivory.

century Chinese porcelain brought from India was still the tableware of the coast but was beginning to be replaced by English print ware and a Continental china, made principally at Saarguemines in Lorraine.

Glazed earthenware from the Islamic world, probably mostly from Persia, was the other luxury ceramic (Plates 2 and 3a). It is in every respect, except occasionally the aesthetic, inferior to porcelain and by the quantity found would appear to have been so regarded in East Africa. The earliest type is *sgraffiato*, the yellow or green glazed ware with patterns incised under the glaze, which was the universal Islamic ware of the Middle Ages. A type with inferior yellow glaze with black geometrical patterns over the same red body, perhaps made at Aden, is characteristic of fourteenth-century levels in Kenya, where *sgraffiato* was never as common as it was in Tanganyika. In the fifteenth century blue-and-white, and blue, green and manganese painted wares with floral patterns, occasionally direct copies of some Chinese designs, came into fashion. A class of small bowls is found from the end of the fourteenth to the end of the seventeenth with floral patterns in blue on a white ground covered by a tin glaze. The acids in the soil have unfortunately eaten away the surface of these bowls and the blue patterns either stand out in low relief or the whole is covered by a loose powdery film. The body is sugary white and the whole class would appear to be related to the Kashan wares of Persia. Also in the middle of the fifteenth century appeared the heavy glossy blue, green and turquoise wide-mouthed, straight-sided monochrome bowls, the only Islamic wares which out-numbered the Chinese wares found with them. They have been found in Fort Jesus but at this time do not seem to have been imported in larger quantities than the polychrome wares which came with them. In the seventeenth and eighteenth centuries, a blue-and-white ware with a kind of Delft body, which was made in Portugal and Spain, was being imported in fair quantities.

Apart from the normal table use, porcelain and glazed earthenware were used as architectural decoration, particu-

C

larly on tombs and mosques, and most of the complete pieces which have survived have come from the walls of collapsed buildings. Few have survived in position: the fallen tomb at Mambrui is exceptional in its frieze of plates below the top (Plate 8*b*). Most were looted by or at the instance of Europeans in the late nineteenth or early twentieth centuries. It was a wasteful form of depredation, as without hydrochloric acid or great patience and delicate handling, it would be extremely difficult to extract them from the masonry matrix without damage. Others served as targets for the local marksman when they began to acquire firearms.

The locally made earthenware is a hard-baked well-made utility article with little pretensions to being anything else. Most of the vessels were cooking pots, storage jars, water pots, eating bowls, beakers, and a few small pots for unguents or condiments. All are either articles for use in the kitchen or by slaves. Two interesting types were the boat-shaped lamps in which a cotton wick floating in ghee would give a flicker of light in a sheltered place, and the flat-bottomed bowls with three flanges or horns which were used as charcoal stoves on dhows. This is a vessel that was introduced from south Arabia towards the end of the fifteenth century, and was subsequently carried across Africa to the Congo by the slave raiders of the nineteenth century. Chronologically there was a distinct change at the end of the fourteenth century when the thin walled vessels of an average thickness of one-tenth of an inch gave way to vessels between one-eighth and one-sixth of an inch thick.

Ornament consisted of a red ochre coat which was sometimes burnished, and incised or pecked ornament which was made up into series of patterns. A large number of variants of these patterns, principally on the cooking pots, have been recorded, particularly from Gedi, and some of the less common varieties may have tribal or functional significance. In the sixteenth and seventeenth centuries there is much less variety and the carinated cooking pot was partially replaced by a bag-shaped vessel with a slightly out-turned neck. Applied ornament occurred but was less common. In the sixteenth century, the practice of painting pots with a dark crimson coat instead of burnishing came in, and there are some local varieties of style. At Ungwana in the north broad radiating strokes were popular, while at Kilwa in the south narrow radiating strokes with stars were the vogue. At Gedi, where tastes were always rather austere, such frivolities did not occur. The world-wide practice of coating the surface of an earthenware vessel with graphite was practised in the south in Tanganyika and Pemba, but not in the part of the coast which is now Kenya.

At the end of the fifteenth century potters' marks appear, indicating the use of a communal kiln and an industry of more than domestic or plantation scale. The marks are simple combinations of strokes or crosses and their purpose would be to distinguish the products of one hand from another. If you share a kiln with your friends they are likely to remain your friends longer if there can be no argument as to whose pots are broken when the kiln is opened. The industry is now on its last legs and is reduced to a few old women making pots by hand rather well, putting them outside the hut when they are dry, and firing them with coconut husk and grass. No kiln, no co-operation and, I am informed, very little profit. Pots with potters' marks have been found in levels in Fort Jesus which are certainly eighteenth century if not later, but no tradition of communal working or even of building of kilns has survived.

A curious and significant lacuna is the complete absence of any sherds which have been used as writing tablets. In Egypt and the Levant broken pieces of jar have been used for notes and accounts—at Lachish in Palestine even for intelligence reports and police court cases—since the middle of the second millennium before Christ when the alphabet began. In East Africa not one inscribed sherd has appeared in fourteen years of excavation. One can understand that the problem of the literate indigent did not occur, but one is surprised that there was always an adequate supply of writing materials.

Among the ceramics found sporadically in the excavations,

35

the fine red wares made in India are of great interest. These were imported at the end of the sixteenth and in the seventeenth centuries, possibly from Diu or Damāo, which are not far from one of the areas where they were made in large quantities. Technically, the ware seems to be identical with well-known Roman Samian, the mark of Roman civilization in western Europe. It was introduced into India in the first centuries of the Christian era when Roman contacts with Broach and other places in Kathiawar were most regular, and was imitated down the centuries by local potters. Only two forms have been reconstructed: one a flask with impressed bulrush millet ornament, found on the floor of the Great Mosque at Gedi, and the other a gourd-shaped bottle with a long neck from a rubbish pit under a Portuguese barrack room in Fort Jesus Mombasa.†

Besides ceramics, the commonest find of the archaeologist is beads, and the East African coast must be one of the most prolific areas of bead-finding anywhere in the world. Notable spots are the beach at Mogadishu, near Tumbatu in Zanzibar, Kilwa in Tanganyika—almost anywhere where there has been a settlement. Ninety per cent of the beads are the small drawn glass beads red, blue, green, yellow and black, the "Trade Wind" beads of the Indian Ocean. They are claimed to have been found in seventh- and eighth-century sites in India and Malaya, but they occur in East Africa in levels from the fourteenth to the eighteenth century. Where they were made has still to be proved, but the west coast of India has a strong claim, and the red beads seem to be the red beads of Negapatam. The loss of Negapatam to the Dutch in 1667 caused a trade crisis in East Africa where the Africans had hitherto refused to take the new lines of European beads which the Portuguese had been trying to introduce. Fortunately, like most people, they accepted the inevitable and the bead trade did not come to an end. In the seventeenth century, similar beads made in Europe began to take their place, and in the eighteenth and nineteenth centuries large

†This was also made in Goa and possibly in Portugal.

coarse blue, white, and red on green beads were imported in large quantities.

The single local manufacture mentioned by the historians or documents is a coarse cotton cloth, but the only products of local industry, besides pottery which have survived, have been beads made from large shells in the form of disks, cylinders and faceted barrels.

One other local craft should be mentioned, the ornamental woodwork. This was expressed in the ebony and inlaid ivory chairs (Plate 5*d*), the silver and ivory ornamental doorlocks (Plate 4), the copper and brass ornamental chests and the carved wooden doors (Plate 5*c*). The doors have patterns of Indian inspiration but there are examples in Mogadishu which are more Arab in style.

The silver work of the coast has never been studied and to what extent it is indigenous is unknown. Siyu had a reputation for silver work.

Glass bottles and bowls, particularly the glass bottles with long necks and wrythen bands used for sprinkling rose water, were imported in quantity. Workmanship was primitive enough and probably most of them came from the glass factories which have been found at Aden. But there were also pieces of moulded, cut and inlaid glass which must have been made at Alexandria, Beirut or Baghdad. In the seventeenth and eighteenth centuries Dutch case bottles, sometimes with pewter caps, were imported, and Guillain in the early nineteenth century draws attention to the demand for glass vessels of all kinds.

Most of the iron implements came from India and the copper eye pencils, toilet utensils and bowls from the Islamic world.

The general picture that emerges is of a well-to-do but not wealthy community, neither luxurious, artistic nor cultured, but in which life was lived according to definite standards of comfort and decorum. The parallels in space and in time are legion, and some are with us today.

The one sign of sophistication is the pungency and cynicism of the Swahili proverbs. High principles are not normally to be found in commercial circles but they are pretended, if not noticeably followed. The Swahili merchants, however, frankly proclaimed the skullduggery of their society:

> Praise the toddy tapper, and he puts water in the toddy.

> Better an Unbeliever that is some use than a Believer who is none.

> A new thing is a joy even though it be an ulcer.

Quite clearly life on the coast had similar problems to those we face today, when we try to conduct our lives and businesses with reasonable efficiency and some modicum of profit in increasingly trying conditions.

2

Somalia

THE OLDEST historical sites on the coast of East Africa
will be found in Somalia, but so far there have been no
excavations to reveal them. The southern shore of the Gulf
of Aden was the land of Punt of the Ancient Egyptians, the
Ophir of the Hebrews, the Berbera and Adel of the Arabs
and Portuguese. It was on this unattractive stretch of coast
that East African commerce was born. The most important
market was a place called Moosullon which has been identified
with Bender Kasim, but a string of harbours and markets
are mentioned in the *Periplus*, showing the extent of business
and the possibilities for the field archaeologist.

The business, however, was not all African. Merchants
from Persia and India also came to these markets with the
products of their countries to exchange them, not necessarily
for those of Africa, but for the products of Egypt and Arabia
which their merchants would bring with them. It was probably through an accident suffered by one of the eastern
merchants that it was discovered that there was profitable
business round the dreadful Cape Guardafui. This had happened sometime before the time of the *Periplus* as the merchants of the Red Sea already were rounding Aromata, the
old name for Guardafui, to reach Opone, the present Hafun
which had become the great market for the East.

The attraction of these markets, apart from their character
of an entrepôt for the produce of the East, was ivory, rhinoceros horn, tortoiseshell, palm oil and, of course, slaves. All

39

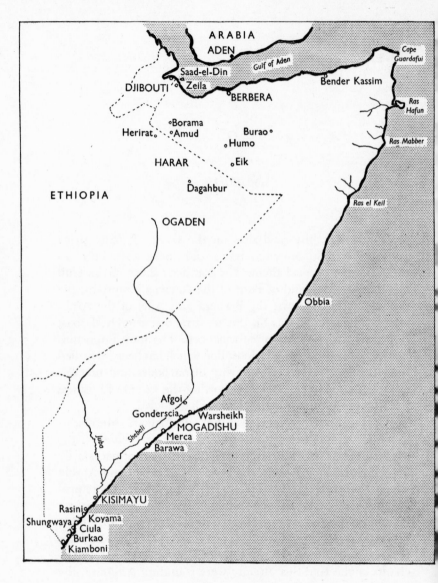

FIG. 2. *Somalia*

these articles that went west and east were paid for with weapons, tools, glass and presumably the cloths of India.

Opone was by no means the limit, even in these early days. The dreary, inhospitable stretch of land between Hafun and Mogadishu had been passed, and the Benadir, "the Land of Harbours", had been reached. The author of the *Periplus* mentions two by name, Serapion and Nikon. Serapion cannot be other than Warsheikh, about thirty miles north of Mogadishu, the second could be either Gonderscia or Merca.

South of Barawa, the country becomes less uniformly barren, and at Juba, considered the boundary between Azania or Berbera and the land of the Zinj, commences the scrub savanna of East Africa.

The shaft of light shone by the *Periplus* burnt out. Nothing comparable was to be written on the coast until the remarkable French Captain Guillain wrote his *Documents et Narrative de Voyages sur la côte de l'Afrique orientale* in the middle of the nineteenth century.

For the identification of place names in the *Periplus* and in the Arab geographers I have followed Guillain. He has the advantage over all other commentators of being a navigator, and of having sailed the same waters in vessels larger, more seaworthy and better equipped, but with the same needs and limitations.

The Arab references to Somalia, apart from Ibn Batuta's visit to Mogadishu, are few and confusing, but there is a Chinese account of the ninth century which is interesting, amusing and, to me, true. The text runs or is said to run (there is always an element of disagreement amongst philologists as to what their unfortunate author or his faithless copyist actually said):

> The country of Po-pa-li is in the south-western sea. The people do not eat any of the five grains but eat only meat. They often stick a needle into the veins of cattle and draw blood which they drink raw, mixed with milk. They wear no clothes except that they cover the parts below their loins with sheepskins. Their women are clean and of proper behaviour. The inhabitants themselves kidnap them, and,

if they sell them to foreign merchants, they fetch several times their price. The country produces only ivory and ambergris.

Well—it is nice to know that the girls were clean and of proper behaviour, whatever that means, and also that their worth was appreciated. The expression "several times their price" is obscure, since presumably the kidnapper paid nothing for them. The dealers were probably middle men in the business, for there is no sanctimonious talk about abundance and cheapness.

The constituents of the population of Somalia in these early days were no different from what they are today, although they have changed in distribution and relative importance. At the beginning of the Christian era, the Somali occupied the strip along the Gulf of Aden, the Galla the country to the south and west, the Bantu the valleys of the Webbe Shebeli and 'the Juba. By the twelfth century the Galla had been pressed southwards and westwards, and Islamized Somali had subjugated the Bantu of the Shebeli and the coastal strip possibly as far south as Merca. The northern limit of Bantuland had been pushed back two hundred and fifty miles, from the Webbe Shebeli to the Juba. In the early seventeenth century the Arabized Ajuran Somali were replaced by the savage Abgal Somali, and the Galla were driven over the Juba, displacing in turn the Bantu, who fled southwards into Kenya. In the middle of the nineteenth century the Somali disposed of the Galla. One of the incidents was a characteristic act of state—a love feast which was converted into a massacre. A group marriage between two tribes was arranged so that the enmity between them would be removed. However, there was no wedding. The seventy-five Galla leaders who had come to attend the ceremony were massacred, and their women and children sold as slaves to the Bantu Pokomo and the outcast Sanya whom they had been oppressing for centuries. The loss of their leaders is a serious matter to a primitive community—to a more advanced society it would be of course the beginning of a golden age—and the Galla have ceased to be a political factor from this time. The place and time is said to have been on the Juba about 1865.

The historical monuments of Somalia, known today, consist of the traces of the old town of Zeila, and the settlement on the nearby island of Saad-el-Din; the group of towns of which Amud appears to have been the most important in the Borama district of the old British Somalia and the related sites of Dagahbur in Ethiopia, and Eik and Humo in the Burao area of Somalia; the remains of mosques and tombs in the old Arab ports of the Benadir; and the phallic pillars reported from Herirat.

The thirteen towns in the Borama area appear from surface finds to have been flourishing in the fifteenth and sixteenth centuries, and were probably destroyed in the victorious campaign of Lebna Dengel, Emperor of Ethiopia, in 1527. The same fate may have been suffered by Eik and Humo, fifty years later, when the threat to Ethiopia from the Galla and Somali was finally removed.

The walls of these buildings are of coursed, roughly shaped stones, stuck together with termite earth. The mosques were naturally the most elaborate and had recessed qiblas and round, cruciform or square pillars, carrying probably a brushwood roof. The phallic pillars stand about six feet high and are similar to those in the Sidamo country of southern Ethiopia. They are ascribed to the Galla and some may be as old as the sixteenth century, when the Galla were driven from the Herirat area.

The towns of the Benadir were more elaborate and, from the surviving monuments of Mogadishu, the most important of them were most prosperous in the thirteenth and fourteenth centuries. In the fifteenth century they were in process of Somalization and by the eighteenth century were in deep decay. Their prosperity must have suffered from the interruption of the trade with the interior, through the Galla invasion of Sidamo and Kafa in the sixteenth century. The mulatto's story in the Book of Pirates (published 1734) belongs to the realm of fancy, and is proof that the coast of East Africa had slipped out of European knowledge. In the nineteenth century they submitted without protest to the easy overlordship of the Albusaid Sultans of Oman. By this time, however, they were at the mercy of unassimilated Somali, and the stranger, imperialist though he might be, was preferable to the neighbour one knew, feared and disliked.

Mogadishu was built, like Gonderscia and Merca, for reasons of defence, on a coral promontory. This is the quarter of Hamarwen which is the core of the old city. Later it spread over the sandy country around, notably towards the north, in front of the anchorage, the quarter known as Shangani.

According to the Swahili tradition, mentioned by Barros, Mogadishu was founded in the tenth century by the Arabs from al Hasa on the Arab shore of the Persian Gulf. However, there is a complete silence in the Arab geographers until the thirteenth century, when it is mentioned in the geographical dictionary of Yakut; its existence is also established by inscriptions.

The name may be derived from "Magaad al Shah", the seat of the Sheikh or Shah. There is nothing necessarily Persian in this expression, but that there was a Persian element among the immigrants is proved by an inscription. In fact, the Shirazi or Persian element on the coast is far better substantiated in Somalia than further south, where there is much more talk about it.

The earliest monument at Mogadishu is the cylindrical minaret of the Great Mosque, which was begun on 1st Muharram 636 (August 14, 1238) (Plate 6a). The dedicatory inscription is in Neskhi script on a background of tendrils. It is placed over the doorway from the mosque which has a pointed arch with a nick at the apex. The old mosque has disappeared and the present building was erected in the nineteenth century.

There are two other old mosques: the mosque of Fakhr al Din and the mosque of Arba' Rukun. The mosque of Fakhr al Din has a curious qibla. In it is a carved marble plaque with a vase hanging by a chain, surrounded by an inscription with the name Haji ibn Muhammad ibn Abdulla, which

44

may be the name of the artist, and the date, the end of the month of Shaaban 667 (April 27–May 6, 1269). The mosque is said to have been founded by the first Sultan of Mogadishu, named Abu Bakr bin Fakhr al Din. The main façade is on the east and has three doorways with carved umbo-shaped bosses over the lintels. There are a few fragments of a carved marble decoration which is said to have been removed to Zanzibar by orders of Seyyid Said. The inside, apart from the qibla, is of little interest; the two tall pillars carrying the roof may be an addition. The building is at present in a very bad state of preservation. When it is restored there will be an opportunity to study the structure of probably the oldest surviving mosque in East Africa.

There exists a curious document of the eighteenth century whose purpose would appear to be the glorification of the position of the Qahtani or Abu Re, the hereditary Qadhis and Khatibs of Mogadishu. In it are the details of the election of the first Sultan, a certain Abu Bakr.

The story relates that the Qahtani supported Abu Bakr's candidature for the sultanate and he promised them the two most important positions in the state. What exactly he had received was the executive, but the judiciary remained in the hands of the Qahtani who could any time reduce his authority to nothing. The fact that Mogadishu was originally governed by heads of families is corroborated by Yakut. The reason for the change of constitution may have been the Somali aggressions. Committees may be the perfect democratic form of government but they have seldom been a success when it comes to war.

The other mosque, Arba' Rukun, in the same quarter has been rebuilt but has a qibla with a dedicatory inscription mentioning the year 667 (A.D. 1268–1269) and the name of the founder Khusru, son of Muhammad al Shirazi.

The old houses of Hamarwen are heavily white-washed, when they are not hopelessly dilapidated. It is impossible to draw any conclusion as to their age but they are probably the houses which Guillain saw in 1846. The level around the Great Mosque and the Mosque of Fakhr al Din has been

45

raised ten feet so that it is necessary to go down steps to enter them. The houses in the immediate vicinity cannot therefore be very old, but the level of the southern part of Hamarwen does not seem to have been so disturbed and the lower parts of some of these houses may go back to the thirteenth century.

The house on the edge of Shangani in which the Museum is housed is an Arab house of the period of Seyyid Barghash. It contains a fine collection of Arabic inscriptions from mosques and tombs, that it is hoped will be adequately published. In quality they are far superior to anything further south. Also in Shangani are two large houses, one with fine carved doorways which appear to be eighteenth century. Nearby is a mosque with a square tower, probably of the same period. At the far northern end is the minaret of the Mosque of Abd al Aziz, which may be the second minaret shown on the sketch of Guillain, and also medieval.

Ibn Batuta visited Mogadishu in 1332 and gives a detailed picture of life in the fourteenth century. The Sultan had come from Berbera and spoke in the "language of Mogadishu", although he could speak Arabic. Since the Sultan's home was in the north, the "language of Mogadishu" is likely to have been a form of Somali rather than Swahili. Ibn Batuta mentions that he was entertained by the Qadhi, as he was a scholar not a merchant. There was a system by which all commercial transactions with foreigners had to be conducted through a local merchant who was also the host. Only an old established foreigner was permitted to house himself and to handle his business directly.

Ibn Batuta describes the visit of the Sultan in state to the mosque, and the court which the Sultan would open and then hand over to his officers of state. Questions which they could not decide themselves would be referred to him, and he would write his decision in chambers, which would then be promulgated in court. The impression that is given is of a petty principality with modest "props", but able to give a reasonable performance.

The Somali infiltration continued. A tomb in the cemetery on the road to Afgoi and the Webbe Shebeli, dated 4 Dhu al Hijjah 766 (August 22, 1365) has the Somali cyclical year as well as the Hejira date.

A number of copper coins, some not unlike the coinage of Kilwa, others with the Tughra of the Turks, have recently come to light and are now being studied. One of the earliest is a coin inscribed Abu Bekr bin Muhammad, and dated 722 (A.D. 1322). The Turkish type coins cannot be earlier than the fifteenth century and may be sixteenth, so presumably Mogadishu was flourishing again.

In 1417 and 1421 Mogadishu was visited on the fifth and sixth voyages of the junks of Cheng Ho, and a brief description of the town is given in which houses four or five stories high are mentioned. The inhabitants are described as quarrelsome and practising archery.

Vasco da Gama touched at Mogadishu on his way back from India in 1499 and describes it as a large town with a palace in the middle. He made no attempt to attack it, and it remained the one major town on the coast that never submitted to the Portuguese. The nearest the Portuguese got to an attack was when Tristan da Cunha appeared off the town in 1507 after the sack of Barawa, but the inhabitants put up such a brave front that he did not attempt to land.

The house of Fakhr al Din disappeared sometime in the sixteenth century and was succeeded by a new dynasty, the Mudhaffarids, who lasted until the middle of the seventeenth century, but the Qahtanis remained the leading family with whom the real authority rested. They were still in power in the nineteenth century when the Sultan of Zanzibar surrendered his rights to Italy. The pen outlasts the sword.

South of Mogadishu are a number of town sites of which Gonderscia, with the adjacent island al Garuin, is the most interesting. It is said to have been destroyed in the wars of the Galla and the Somali some time in the eighteenth century, but it may have ceased to be a relatively civilized centre some time earlier.

Beyond Gonderscia is Merca. The old town is largely in ruins, as it was over a hundred years ago, but the ruins appear of no great age. Around the qibla of the Great Mosque is an

47

inscription giving a date in the Hejira year 1018, which corresponds to 1609 but the mosque appears to be later. Outside the walls is the mosque of Sheikh Osman, also dated by an inscription to the year 1560. Merca is mentioned by Idrisi, Ibn Said and Yakut but there is nothing visible today which could be as early as the twelfth or thirteenth century. Ibn Said describes it as the centre of the Hadiya, presumably the Hawiya, and if so this is important evidence as to the early penetration of the coastal strip by the Somali. In the eighteenth century it suffered a series of misfortunes. It was sacked first by the Biemal Somali as reprisal for the rape of a Somali girl, then by Sultan Yusif of Guébroun for having too easily submitted to his enemy the Garra Saltan of Bardera, and finally by Abdulla bin Ahmed al Mazrui on his way to Bombay in 1816. By this time it must have been at a low ebb and accepted the nominal protection of Seyyid Said with relief.

A hundred miles further south is Barawa, which is the same type of settlement as Mogadishu and Merca but has retained some of its Bantu-Arab as opposed to Somali-Arab character. A form of Swahili is still spoken, "Kimbalawi", although in Guillain's day Somali was the habitual language. Visitors of the nineteenth century commented on the amiability of the inhabitants of Barawa, as compared with the bellicosity of those of Merca and Mogadishu. The name would seem to be the same as the Berouat of Idrisi, which is described as being at the end of the country of the Kafirs. If by Kafirs are meant Bantu as opposed to Galla and Somali, this would be a not unreasonable position, since the northern frontier of Bantuland had been pushed south from the latitude of Mogadishu by the invasion of the Hadiya. In the history of Kilwa it is mentioned with Mogadishu as being already in existence when the Shirazi ships arrived. In the Great Mosque is an inscription of the ninth-century Hejira (the fifteenth century of the Christian era), and another very dubious, said to be twelfth century. Otherwise there is nothing at Barawa except an isolated tower on the shore to suggest its antiquity.

48

6(a) Minaret of Great Mosque, Mogadishu, built A.D. 1238

(b) Palace of Pate. Probably eighteenth century.

7. Qibla and minbar of Great Mosque, Ungwana. Sixteenth century.

Unlike the other towns of the coast, Barawa never had a sheikh or sultan but was ruled by a number of heads of clans. In 1506 it was stormed by Tristan da Cunha. The citizens of Barawa fought more valiantly than any other town on the coast. The fiercest fighting took place in the square in front of the Great Mosque and the Portuguese lost forty men before resistance crumbled. After the fight the city was sacked with great brutality, but in the withdrawal many of the soldiers, including those who had behaved worst after the battle, were drowned. With all their faults, the Portuguese did not hide their misdeeds and expressed satisfaction when Providence stepped in as an avenger of the crimes which they committed. They seldom denied or tried to cover up the enormities which someone should have had the guts to stop. Barawa submitted to Nuno da Cunha at Malindi in 1529, and again to Antonio de Albuquerque at Pate in 1728. On the latter occasion she hoped to get help against the Galla but she was never subject to Portugal. Later she accepted the suzerainty of Oman, but in 1824 put herself under the unauthorized protection of Captain Owen. On the withdrawal of the British representative at Mombasa, the Protectorate lapsed and Barawa returned to her Omani allegiance. Barawa seems to have been the last settlement which could be called a town, and in fact no monuments have been reported until the estuary of the Juba is reached. On the string of islands between Kisimayu and Burkao (Port Durnford), and on the mainland as far as the Kenya frontier are the remains of pillar tombs, other tombs and occasional mosques. None of these settlements was of any size or consequence, and they represent, I believe, the lower stratum of the culture of the coast. The monuments, tombs and mosques are similar to those on the Kenya sites.

The tombs can be divided into those with tall tapering pillars, such as Ciula which closely resembles the pillar at Uwani in Kenya, even to the Canton jar on top of it, and those with stubby pillars which can be paralleled at Kiunga. There are groups of similar ruins at Ngumi, Koyama and Kiamboni. The finest, perhaps the finest of all pillar tombs,

D

is at Burkao. The ruined mosques are not impressive except the little gem of a qibla at Rasini. This has an elaborately carved façade which recalls the qibla at Mgangani near Gedi. No excavations have yet been carried out and it is possible that some of these sites may be earlier than the fourteenth century. The present inhabitants, the Bajun, are not an historically minded people and know nothing about them.

These ruins may be the remains of the old Arab-African state of Shungwaya, whose headquarters were about Burkao. On the Arab side, Shungwaya has a certain fabulous character —the white flag flown by Swahili dhows is said to be the flag of the Sultan of Shungwaya. It, however, survives in the traditions of all the Nyika tribes, who claim to have been settled at Shungwaya and to have been driven from their homes by the Galla, at a period which can be reckoned as the late sixteenth or early seventeenth century.

The absence of impressive buildings may perhaps be explained by the fact that these were settlements with a largely subsistence economy, as they are today. The lack of contact with the larger world inspired no thoughts of emulation or grandeur, which was the motive behind the mosques of Mogadishu and Kilwa. In a dull equality and fraternity, there was no impulse to live better than one's fellows. One is surprised at the element of posthumous discrimination implied in the erection of a pillar tomb, but a tomb, even a pillar tomb, is an easier thing to build than a house.

In the seventeenth century the Portuguese drew Bajun and Somali mercenaries from Shungwaya and Ciula, and in the eighteenth century the Sultans of Pate raided the small settlements along the coast. The inhabitants of these islands are said to have had the useful gift of binding the winds. A pleasant story is told of the last slave raid in the late nineteenth century, when a slaving dhow was held until the British District Commissioner from Kisimayo could arrive and arrest the raiders.

3

The Lamu Archipelago

THE BOUNDARY between the former Italian colony of
Somalia and the colony of Kenya was originally fixed at the
Juba, with Kisimayo inside the British administered territory. After the First World War it was altered and the whole
of the Juba valley was transferred to Italy.

The present (1962) boundary is at the promontory known
as Ras Kiamboni, which is crowned by a striking pillar tomb
and the ruins of a considerable settlement. Six miles south is
the small walled town of Ishikani with more tombs, including
a pillar tomb. About half a mile from the town is a rectangular
tomb, or rather a mausoleum, surrounded with panels of
asymmetric geometrical patterns (Fig. 3). Islamic as well as
Christian art is descended from the adult, rational arts of
the classical world, or the equally mature art of Persia. But
the Ishikani panels look back, some would say look forward,
to an artistic world in which apparent symmetry and rele-
vance have been superseded by an esoteric balance and
urgency which only the initiated can appreciate. There must
be other examples, but they have not yet been recorded. The
nearest to them is the cross in the mihrab recess of the mosque
of Nossy Manja in Madagascar. There is no reason to suppose that the tomb is any less Muslim than the surrounding
tombs.

Six miles further south is Kiunga, with a ruined mosque
and a number of panelled tombs. The principal settlement
was once on the island opposite, Kiungamwini. It was

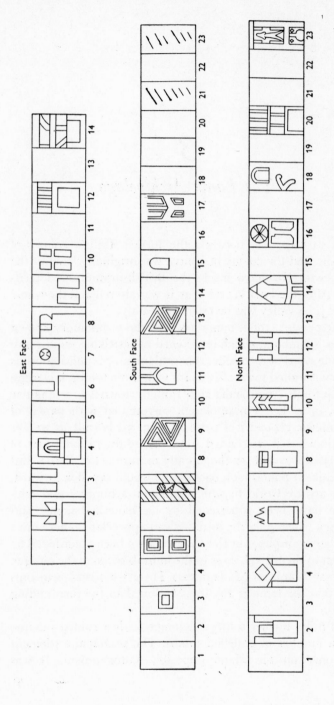

FIG. 3. *A diagram of the carved panels of a tomb at Ishikani. The west face is undecorated*

bombarded by the British frigate after the murder of a Scottish naval officer engaged in the "brutal" suppression of the brutal slave trade. The population then moved or perhaps returned to the mainland. On the island is a pillar tomb of unusual design, said to have been erected over the grave of this officer. On the hill overlooking the bay and the island is the District Office, a single-storied building, one of a group which was built in the early twentieth century, when it was considered desirable that the representative of government should live over his shop and not in suburban privacy.

South of Kiunga a long chain of small islands runs down the coast, similar to the chain between Kisimayo and Burkao, leaving a safe channel navigable by sailing or poling almost all the way to Manda Bay and the Lamu Archipelago. The islands are uninhabited but on the mainland are a number of settlements, where the minor products of westernization, such as matches, tinned milk, cigarettes, cloth and kerosene can be obtained. The population is divided between agriculturists and seafarers in a proportion of about one-third to two-thirds. The sources of income are mangrove poles, dried fish and illicit ivory; millet, maize and sweet potatoes provide the daily bread. No one makes very much money but there is no starvation. It is subsistence living at its best—"the daily wants of every day, the toil of every day supplied". Those who do not like it and believe that life may have something more to offer, go to Lamu and then Mombasa.

There is one considerable old site, Omwe, which is mentioned in the Pate history and later gave its name to one of the Nine Tribes of Mombasa. Today it is buried in thick bush, but the small township of Mambore with its creek is only a quarter of a mile from the north gate. The best preserved and most interesting monument is an unusual type of pillar tomb with a frieze ornament of inverted shields, known as the Tomb of the She Buruhan. About half a mile from the settlement is another pillar tomb of the tapered type, similar to those at Kiamboni and Ishikani.

The track winds southwards through the savanna among baobabs and occasional mangoes, or descends into swamps,

53

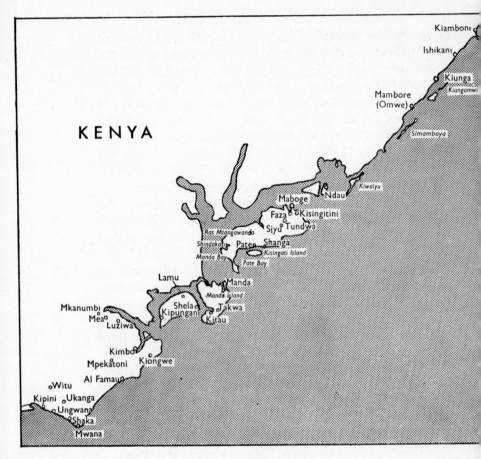

FIG. 4. *Lamu Archipelago*

where a fault in the coral has caused a breaking back of the
mainland and a deposit of soil in the salt water to promote
the growth of mangroves.

The last of the islands, Kiwaiyu, rises to a height of some
sixty feet. From the top it is possible to see the whole extent
of the Lamu Archipelago. Nearest is Ndau, the smallest
of the islands, with two villages engaged in boat building.
Beyond is an uninhabited mangrove-covered sandbank,
then the long, low outline of Pate and in the distance Manda
and Lamu, with their tall sandhills built up by the north-

54

east monsoon, which blows strongly for most of the day between November and February.

These islands would appear to be the Pyralaon Islands,
the islands of the "People of Fire" of the *Periplus*. The name
may come from the common practice of burning the bush
before the rains in the early part of the year, either to improve
the grazing or to prepare the ground for cultivation. If this
explanation is correct, the population of the islands must
have been much greater than it is today to make sufficiently
good fires to earn the monopoly of the name.

Pate is the largest of the islands with three small townships,
Pate, Faza and Siyu, besides a number of smaller settlements,
such as Tundwa and Kizingitini. The coral core of the island
is fringed with mangrove swamps, which in places cover
large areas; the townships of Faza and Siyu are almost completely surrounded by them. There are coconut plantations
near the main towns but the principal product is tobacco,
mostly for making snuff.

The most important of the three was Pate which, according
to its own history, played a great part on the coast in the
fourteenth century. It is unfortunate that it is never referred
to by the Arab geographers or indeed by the historian of
Kilwa. It is first mentioned in the sixteenth century by the
Portuguese. In the late seventeenth and eighteenth centuries
it was a place of consequence, as important as Mombasa
and Mogadishu. The town is situated on the flank of a ridge
sloping down to a mangrove filled creek. A narrow winding
stream finds its way to the sea about half a mile from the
town, and is navigable by small boats at high tide. The creek
passes the town and opens up into a wide flat, which at high
springs is covered with water, some of which comes from
Manda Bay on the other side, the western side, of the island.
The mouth faces the open sea, which is here due south not
due east, and is protected to some extent by the island of
Kisingati. The creek must at one time have been much more
open, although no large dhows or galleons could ever have
got very close. As a place of commerce it was always greatly
inferior to Lamu, and one heartily agrees with the Sultan

Bwana Mkuu bin Abubekr (1454–89), who resided much at Lamu and insisted on all dhows discharging their cargo there instead of Pate. It is strange that after the conquest of Faza in the twelfth century the people of Pate did not move out and take up their residence in the best harbour of the island. Today the normal approach is on foot from the anchorage of Ras Mtangawanda on the north side of the island, about forty minutes walk away.

The history of Pate from the late sixteenth century onwards comes from many sources. Unfortunately, the sources seldom agree and never on actual dates, even if they are both Muslim, while the story as revealed in the Portuguese and Pate sources is so diverse that it could easily be about two different places. The Portuguese records, mostly official documents (painful though it must be to some people) inspire the most confidence. The Pate history omits incidents which would be discreditable to national pride or even which occurred outside the islands.

The Omani capture of Mombasa (1660) and the siege of Fort Jesus (1696–98), in both of which Pate played a prominent part, are overlooked but there is a reference to Pate interventionists in the Mombasa revolt of 1729. The two visits of the Turkish Captain Mirale Bey (1586 and 1589), the prolonged campaign of Almeida (1678–79) and the final Portuguese expedition of 1728–29 are all ignored. There is no mention of the executions of two Sultans of Pate in 1603 and 1679. The one account of military operations on the island is on the occasion of an attack from the direction of Shindakasi, an anchorage at the north-west corner, which is almost certainly the expedition of the exuberant Francisco Seixas de Cabreira, Captain of Mombasa. But true to form the humiliation of the destruction of the town walls is not mentioned. On the other hand, there are frequent references to the Portuguese settlers at Dondo or Tundwa, and the fact that certain sultans were on good terms with the Portuguese is recorded without reproach. They learnt from them the useful art of excavating wells with the use of gunpowder, and the equally useful and no less harmful device of custom duties.

Five versions of the history of Pate exist, the original is said to have been destroyed in the British bombardment of Witu in 1890. Four of these are derived from a gentleman known as Bwana Kitini or Muhammad bin Fumo Omar al Nabahan, a scion of the princely house of Pate. Bwana Kitini was a colourful type who had taken a prominent part in the Witu campaign and is said to have killed Sultan Fumo Bakari in true renaissance style with a poisoned hookah, hoping for the reward offered but never paid. In the latter part of his life he became the respected oracle of local history and tradition to whom Captain Stigand, Miss Werner and anyone else would go to hear about the past. Of the various versions, the Stigand version is the fullest and has the best stories, but the dates and names of the sultans are the most confused. The most convincing in these respects is the Cusack version in the District Office at Lamu, but this is interrupted at the beginning of the seventeenth century and never quite recovers its old form. The fifth version has never been published.

The ruling house of Pate was of the clan of the Nabahan from the tribe of Azd who were the *maliks* or rulers of Oman from A.D. 1154–1406. The founder of the line was Suleiman ibn Suleiman, who arrived in the year H. 600 (A.D. 1203). He found Arabs already established under a ruler named Ishak al Battawi, whose daughter he married. These Arabs may have been part of a wave of immigrants, under a Suleiman and a Said, who had been driven out of Oman by Al Hajjaj ibn Yusuf, the famous viceroy of Iraq at the end of the seventh century, and who settled in East Africa.

The new sultans were an aggressive lot, and by the beginning of the fourteenth century had made themselves masters of the whole archipelago. A Sultan Omar bin Muhammad (A.D. 1331–48) is claimed to have conquered the whole coast from Warsheikh to the Kerimba Isles off Cape Delgado. The title Yumbe, borne by small chiefs of the Mrima (Tanganyika coast) and used also in Kenya as a term of respect for headman, is said to refer to the Palace at Pate and to be derived from the household slaves of the Palace who were given posts in the conquered territories. However, there is no corroboration of this achievement from the Kilwa history or any other source. The son or brother of Omar, Muhammad, his successor was an altogether different type. In the Werner version it is said:

> And he was extremely fond of money and of trade, and caused men to make voyages in ships and sent them to India and traded there and he had great good luck as regards money.

In the Stigand version this satisfactory state of affairs is confirmed, and it is said that he built vessels called *gharabs*, the present day *jahazis*. This is interesting as it suggests the date of the construction on the coast of ocean-going dhows. The prosperity of Pate continued through the fourteenth and fifteenth centuries and included the discovery of an island with silver deposits, which seems pretty improbable.

In the sixteenth century the sultans regularly submitted to the Portuguese and were able to wriggle out of most of the disagreeable consequences of their reluctance to pay tribute and their intrigues with the Turks. The Sultan of Pate was fortunate to be a witness, not a companion of the Sheikh of Lamu when he was hanged and quartered with due ceremony at Pate on April 6, 1589. Subsequently, relations seem to have improved, and when the Franciscan Gaspar de São Bernardino visited Pate in 1606 he found eighteen Portuguese settlers in and around the town and an Augustinian priest at Faza. It appeared to him that everyone was on excellent terms with everybody else. The Portuguese at Dondo or Tundwa near Faza are mentioned in the Pate history as having intervened on behalf of a revolted sheikh of Siyu. Later the situation deteriorated and a Portuguese judge, Pedro Alvares Pereira, reported on the bad behaviour of the Portuguese and set up machinery for the settlement of disputes between them and the local inhabitants.

The Sultan, however, assisted Dom Jeronimo, Sultan of Mombasa, after his flight in 1632 and was made to pay a heavy fine as well as to send ships to look for him in the Comoros. In addition the masterful Cabreira forced all the towns on the islands, except Faza, to pull down their walls. A customs house was set up to collect dues from ships that did not want to go to Mombasa, and in 1643 there was still a Portuguese factor living at Pate. But by the middle of the century Pate had assumed the place of Mombasa in the sixteenth century as the leader of the Swahili freedom movement, and Faza the place of the co-operating Malindi. There was one difference, important enough to the sheikh of Faza, which was that the Portuguese were seldom able to protect him and he spent most of his time in Goa.

On August 9, 1678 the Viceroy of Goa, Pedro Almeida, arrived off Pate with a strong expedition. The town walls had been rebuilt and it was not until December 14 that it capitulated. On the excuse that the treaty had been broken by the failure to collect the fine of thirty thousand crusados, the Sultan and the sheikhs of Siyu, Manda and Lamu, for good measure, were executed. The Portuguese did not enjoy their ill-used success for long. The arrival of four Arab vessels from Oman brought reinforcements, and after three days of furious street fighting the Portuguese were forced to withdraw, leaving behind a large pile of looted ivory. The sites of the Portuguese forts and camps and the points of disembarkation are uncertain, but they were probably in the broken ground covered with bush to the east of the town traversed by the Siyu road, under the lee of Kisingati Island. The people of Pate fought more stoutly in this battle than they had ever done before and the policy of frightfulness used by the Viceroy did not produce the expected, often quite rightly expected, return of ready submission.

Eight years later in July 1687 the Portuguese returned under the Captain of Mombasa, João Antunes Portugal. The fighting men of Pate were away on a foray against Shungwaya, and when Antunes Portugal bought the town guard of sixty Galla, the game was up. The Sultan submitted, paid a fine of seventeen thousand crusados and was sent to Goa. There he signed a suitable treaty, but was retained in Goa while the Portuguese were building a fortress for a hundred soldiers at Pate and a blockhouse at Faza for a post of twenty. In fact neither task got very far; six weeks after the engineer arrived, Arab reinforcements from Oman appeared and the Portuguese fled. The unfortunate Sultan left in Goa, despairing of getting back, attempted with his companions to escape on the night of Christmas 1688 but was killed in a gallant fight with the Portuguese guards. This Sultan is said in the Kilwa history to have been, not the Sultan, but his cousin of the same name, Bwana Tamu, a troublesome pretender to the throne whom the Sultan was glad to have deported. It seems impossible for the Portuguese Captain to have been willingly deceived, since he had the watchful sheikh of Faza at hand. It is, however, possible that he saw in Bwana Tamu the likelihood of a useful dependent, whose position, doubtful though it was, had been officially recognized.

A change from the tale of battle is the account of the circumstances of the making of the famous ivory horn or *siwa*, now in the District Commissioner's residence at Lamu. These horns were finely carved musical instruments which were blown on ceremonial occasions (Plate 5*a* and *b*). Mwana Darini, daughter of the Sultan and the wife of the unfortunate Bwana Tamu who had been sent to Goa, grieved greatly for her husband and waited for him to return. But after three years, realizing he would not come back, she decided to make a circumcision feast for her son. Her father, the old Sultan, was dead and had been succeeded by her brother, who was shortly after murdered by an uncle, Ahmad bin Abubekr, who became Sultan. The Sultan heard of his niece's proposed party and, like a society hostess, decided to give a party on the same day in order to steal the guests and, more important, to get the horn. These horns were a great mark of distinction and privilege and are mentioned in connexion with all the towns of the coast. Mwana Darini's feast would obviously not be the success she wanted without a horn and she no less obviously would not have it if the Sultan wanted it. Fortunately, she found a craftsman of the name of Mwenye Bayayi who could make horns. A substitute was produced at the party as a surprise and everyone

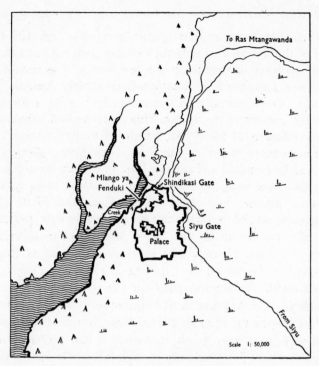

FIG. 5. *Plan of Pate in the 17th century*

admired it, so the hostess was not shamed. Later the other horn, apparently the only other one, was lost at sea and so Mwana Darini's horn became the *siwa* of Pate. Sultan Ahmad who was probably the Sultan of the great siege of Mombasa, abdicated after seven years of drought, which he took as a hint of divine displeasure, and was succeeded by Bwana Tamu the Great. This person is said to have destroyed the Arab settlements on the Tana, Shaka and Waungwana wa Mashaa (probably the old Hoja).

The relations of Pate and the Portuguese did not cease altogether. The people of Pate liked the Arabs of Oman considerably less on closer acquaintance than when they were "fighting friends". The Arab garrison of Pate was massacred and the Sultan Bwana Tamu, alarmed at possible reprisals, invited the Portuguese to come back to the Swahili coast.

In 1728 they were fortunately able to do this, and with the help of the Sultan and without fighting they regained their whole position in the space of a few weeks. A governor of Pate was appointed, a Brazilian-born *fidalgo*, Antonio de Albuquerque Coelho, who commenced to build a fortress with the consent of the Sultan. However, the bad behaviour of his colleague at Mombasa, which led to a revolt and the confinement of the Portuguese in Fort Jesus, effectually upset all he could do at Pate. On June 13 the pro-Arab party, who had now won over the Sultan, fired the town in the Moscow manner and withdrew to Faza and Siyu. The Portuguese retired to the beach near the factory gate, perhaps near the remains of the gate called *Mlango ya Fenduki* (Gate of the Customs House). The loyal sheikh Daud of Faza, who had accompanied the expedition, was able to stop any attack on the Portuguese position, but it was so obviously untenable that Antonio de Albuquerque decided to retire, and on August 14, 1729 set sail for Goa. No traces of the unfinished fortress have yet been found; it had probably not progressed very far. Curiously enough this whole memorable episode is totally ignored in the Pate history.

The expulsion of the Portuguese from Fort Jesus and the preoccupation of the Omanis in civil war and resisting Persian aggression left a power vacuum in East Africa which the sultans of Pate and the Mazrui governors of Mombasa competed to fill. At the beginning the sultans of Pate were the stronger and their authority, nominal or otherwise, extended northwards as far as the Juba and southwards to Kilifi. It also included, how and by what right we do not know, the rich island of Pemba, which they were later forced to surrender to Mombasa.

The change of dynasty in Oman from the Yaarubis to the Albusaid had its repercussions in East Africa, and the son of Bwana Tamu, Bwana Bakari, was killed with an Omani garrison in an anti-foreign uprising. Soon after, civil war broke out between Mwana Khadija, the sister and successor of a Sultan Abu Bekr, and a Sultan Omar who was her vizier. It lasted for ten years from c. 1763–73, and is said to have ruined the state of Pate.

Fumo Madi who reigned from c. 1777–1809 was the last great Sultan of Pate. He acknowledged the distant authority of the Sultan of Oman and made no attempt to regain Pemba, which had been taken off the Mombasa governors by the Omani governor of Zanzibar. The history of Pate states bluntly and pleasurably:

> Then ruled Bwana Fumomadi, his name was Sultan Muhammad bin Abu Bakr Bwana Mkuu bin Abu Bakr. After his succession his subjects wanted to make strife; he fought with them and defeated them and seizing forty people, two of them his own brothers, cut their throats like goats on the roof so that the blood ran down the gutters into the street. There was peace; nobody else arose to cause trouble, and he ruled very joyfully until his death in the year of the Hejira 1224 (A.D. 1809). Nor did a prince rule like him again.
>
> (Werner).

After the death of Fumo Madi, there was the usual strife over the succession and Pate fell under the influence of the Mazrui of Mombasa. This influence did not last long but waned with the increasing interest taken in the coast by Seyyid Said, Sultan of Oman, and disappeared with the final surrender of Mombasa in 1837. The doomed Nabahani had continued their internal dissensions, blind to the fate of the Mazrui. The Omani candidate was, however, normally in power at Pate and the unsuccessful candidate in exile at Kau on the mainland. So far as opposition to the Sultan was concerned, the Sheikhs of Siyu played a more distinguished part, but the Nabahani were involved in their ruin. In 1856, the Sheikh of Siyu attempted to put an end to the town by killing the men and stealing the women and children. But the elders of Pate—the Sultan had fled to the mainland— put up a stout fight at the Siyu Gate on the hill, and the Shindakasi Gate, presumably near the track from Mtanga- wanda at the back of the creek, and the attack was repulsed with great slaughter.

Two years later the new Sultan, Ahmad Simba, seeing

that the spirit of defeat was triumphant in Pate, abandoned his capital and went to Kau on the Tana, where he set up the new principality of Ozi. With him went many of his relatives and followers. The present huddle of squalid houses is the result of the departure of the sheikhly Nabahani and the relegation of their once proud capital city to the descendants of their menials.

The great town (for East Africa) of Pate has lost all its former glory (Plate 6b). The walls which were still standing at the beginning of the century, have largely been destroyed for lime. They are not likely to be older than the middle of the seventeenth century and may be considerably later. The best preserved stretches are along the ridge beside the Siyu Gate, the gate or tower *Mlango ya Fenduki* and the rounded bastions along the creek. The Palace, the scene of the massacre of the forty nobles, is in ruins (Plate 6b). A few years ago the Great Mosque was destroyed and a new mosque built on the site, through the indifference of the inhabitants and the reluctance of the builders to use their God-given intelligence in combining the old with the new.

No excavations have yet been carried out at Pate, but the Palace and the Siyu Gate show evidence of several rebuildings. In the Museum at Fort Jesus is a tombstone of a Sultan Omar bin Muhammad, apparently the great conqueror of the coast in the thirteenth century (Plate 11a). There is one old dated tomb in Pate of a Sultan Muhammad bin Abu Bakr bin Sultan Bwana Mkuu who died in H.1024 (A.D. 1624). It is not easy to fit this Sultan into the lists, but it would appear most likely that he is the Muhammad bin Abu Bakr bin Muhammad of Werner, "who made a treaty with some Europeans who took some of their towns". This might be a reference to the settlement enforced by Tomé de Sousa Coutinho after the Turkish raids (1589), by which Pate seems to have lost temporally her position of dominance on the island. The two oldest surviving mosques are Bwana Tamu, possibly the Bwana Tamu the Great of the Luis de Mello expedition of 1728, and Bwana Bakari his successor. They therefore belong to the first half of the eighteenth century.

8(a) Tomb of the Cross Fitché, Ungwana. Late fifteenth century.

(b) Pillar Tomb, Mambrui, decorated with porcelain plates. Late sixteenth century.

9(a) Pillar Tomb, Malindi. Early fifteenth century.
(b) Pillar Tomb, Mnarani. Early fifteenth century.

The sherds of porcelain and glazed earthenware in the vicinity of the ruins are similar to those unearthed on all sites in East Africa, and I have not found any pieces earlier than the fourteenth century.

The position of Pate as master of the island has now been assumed by its old enemy Faza, which has become the administrative centre under a mudir, or assistant district officer. Of the three old towns, Pate, Faza and Siyu, Faza is the most accessible and, even at low tide, can be reached in half an hour's easy walk on sand from the anchorage at the mouth, called Rasini.

The original Faza was conquered by Sultan Muhammad in the thirteenth century, and in the Pate history is said to have remained unoccupied until the settlement of the Bajun from the mainland in the time of Bwana Tamu at the beginning of the eighteenth century. This is of course untrue, because Faza played an active part in the island politics of the sixteenth and seventeenth centuries.

The second, the sixteenth-century town of Faza, known to the Portuguese as Ampaza, is first mentioned in connexion with the raid of Mirale Bey in 1586. The following year it paid a terrible price for its support of Mirale Bey and for the murder of a wounded Portuguese. There are conflicting accounts of what happened. One is that the town was stormed and every living creature in it butchered; the other that most of the inhabitants ran away into the bush when the Portuguese landed. They agree in saying that the Sheikh Stambuli and a small band fought to the last, a most unusual phenomenon in Swahili warfare, and he attained the unintended honour of having his head sent to Goa for exhibition. The town was burnt after the doors had been looted by the people of Pate and the coconut palms cut down, but these punishments neither caused the site to be abandoned nor affected the relations between the inhabitants and the Portuguese. On the contrary, the new Sheikh of Faza and his successors were the only friends of the Portuguese on the Island. Without becoming Christians they permitted a chapel to be built, tolerated the Portuguese settlers at Faza and were always

E

ready to sneak on their colleagues of Pate and Siyu whenever they had a chance. For this reason, their sheikh or a member of his family—it was not always possible to know the precise standing at the moment of the members of a sheikhly family—was frequently an exile in Goa or in a camp outside Pate. The most distinguished of them was the Bwana Daud who took part in the expedition of 1678 and 1687, and his cousin, the heroic defender of Fort Jesus in 1697, and the friend of the beleaguered garrison of Pate in 1729.

In the eighteenth century Faza is seldom mentioned; in the nineteenth, it served as a base for Seyyid Said and Seyyid Majid in their expeditions against Siyu. With the eclipse of Pate and Siyu, it was able to develop and in the second half of the nineteenth century was ruled by a slippery individual called Mzee bin Saif, who was recognized as chief of the Bajuns as far as Port Durnford, until he was deposed by the Protectorate government.

Today the antiquities of Faza consist of the ruins of two mosques; Bwana Shali Fatani, which has a fine trefoliated mihrab; and Mwenye Ngombe, which has a panelled façade. Bwana Shali Fatani may be eighteenth century while Mwenye Ngombe is perhaps early nineteenth. The Great Mosque has been rebuilt, no doubt over a much earlier building. No excavations have yet been carried out, and it is possible that there may be sherd evidence of the thirteenth-century town, but there is nothing to suggest that in the past it rivalled either Pate or Siyu.

The inhabitants of Faza are more hard-working and more go-ahead than those of the other towns, but I cannot say I have seen any traces of the Portuguese blood which were observed by Stigand in 1912.

About two miles from Faza on the ridge along the middle of the island is the village of Tundwa, the Dondo of the Portuguese. There are no traces of the Portuguese settlement today, although in the middle of the village is a masonry pillar about ten feet high, whose significance I have been unable to discover. The ruined mosque on the way from Faza is nineteenth century.

The third town, Siyu, is at the end of a long winding creek with a muddy unpleasant bottom. It is supposed only to have been founded at the time of Muhammad Fumomadi of Pate, who was a contemporary of the Portuguese. It was in existence in 1589, as its Sultan attended the execution ceremony at Pate. In 1606 it was described by Gaspar de S. Bernardino as the largest town in the island, larger apparently than Pate. At one time the Portuguese intervened to protect it from Pate, but subsequently it fell under the influence of Pate and in 1637 suffered the demolition of its walls. During the rest of the seventeenth and in the eighteenth century it kept out of politics. It was during the time of Sheikh Mataka and his son that it enjoyed a brief period of political importance during the last struggles of the Swahili towns against the Omani government.

In 1856 a large expedition landed at Faza under the Omani Amir Hamid to take Siyu, which had now become the centre of opposition. The town was blockaded, the dhows in the creek being turned over to serve as forts. Sheikh Mataka, feeling that the end was near, consulted a sherif, who in turn consulted his grandfather, Sharif Mwenyi Said, who was buried in a tomb at Siyu. The gentleman in the tomb reassured his grandson; the troops of Siyu carried out a counter attack, killed the Amir, captured his guns and stormed the dhow redoubts. Seyyid Said gave up the campaign and sailed away.

Subsequently the two sons of Sheikh Mataka allied themselves with Seyyid Majid, the successor of Said, against the Sultan of Pate, and a fort was built at Siyu which was garrisoned by Majid's soldiers. But in 1863 Sheikh Muhammad, the second son of Mataka, turned out the soldiers, pulled down the fort and allied himself with the Sultan of Pate, Ahmad Simba. The war was resumed, but this time fortune changed. Sultan Ahmad fled to Kau on the mainland, Siyu was blockaded and Sheikh Muhammad submitted. Later he unwisely presented himself at Zanzibar, where he was arrested and locked up in Fort Jesus, Mombasa for the rest of his life. The fort was rebuilt and stands today at the

67

end of Siyu creek, one of the most picturesque monuments on the coast.

Siyu retains part of its town walls, two mosques, and a number of houses with plastered walls and rows of niches like columbaria. The niches served to display, amongst other articles, the Chinese porcelain which has been collected over all periods. None of these monuments, except possibly the lower parts of the walls, are likely to be older than the nineteenth or late eighteenth century. Outside the walls there is an interesting tomb half buried in rubble and earth, consisting of a small chamber with a cylindrical pillar at the east end and crosses at the corners, which may be as early as the seventeenth century.

The ruling family of Siyu was the Famau, one of the most distinguished families of the islands and notable for the number of poets and poetesses it produced. The *Utendi* of Mwana Kupona, written by the wife of Bwana Mataka, is one of the most beautiful Swahili poems. The inhabitants had a reputation for silver work which is only now dying out. There was a very high infestation of *trifalaria* (elephantiasis) from the mosquitoes which bred in shells in the mangrove swamps. This is now being eradicated, after much local opposition, by the wholesale spraying of the houses.

On the opposite side of the island, reached by a muddy walk through the mangrove swamps, are the ruins of a settlement known as Shanga. It is the scene of a story with an extraordinary Christian flavour. During the capture of Shanga by Sultan Muhammad of Pate in the thirteenth century a maiden was pursued by a soldier. She prayed for the ground to open and swallow her, which it obligingly did, leaving only the border of her robe visible. The soldier, when he saw what had happened, gave up the profession of arms and led a devout life till he died, tending the shrine which Sultan Muhammad put up over the spot. Today there is a small mosque with a pillar over the qibla, as at Takwa, and some houses, none likely to be earlier than the fifteenth century, but the site is covered in very thick bush and there must be other buildings. It is said to have been occupied again temporarily by the people of Siyu when they were in fear of Galla raids. The site is on the open sea with a wide stretch of sand at low tide protected to some extent from the north-east monsoon by Kisingati Island outside Pate.

Separated from Pate by a channel about half a mile wide is the island of Manda, now only intermittently inhabited by fishermen. Once it was the site of three small towns; Manda or Mandra, Takwa and Kitau, which are said to have been conquered by Sultan Omar of Pate in the thirteenth century.

Manda is described as one of the oldest settlements on the coast. Its people were called "The Wearers of Gold" and were noted for their snobbery. The town was taken by Sultan Omar of Pate as a result of a slight which the representative of the fisherman considered he had received by not being asked to a council meeting. The injured gentleman felt that his democratic rights had been flouted and arranged for the gate to be opened to the enemy at night. Most of the inhabitants were carried off to Pate, but some escaped and with the refugees from Takwa and Kitau fled to Lamu. Subsequently they were allowed to settle at Shela, on condition that they built no stone buildings, or rather buildings with stone roofs which could be used as fortresses. The people of Lamu wished to remain unchallenged on their island and were taking no risks.

The site was reoccupied and repeopled with Bajun from the mainland and was in existence in the sixteenth century. It was heavily involved in the revolt against the Portuguese at the time of the second expedition of Mirale Bey in 1589. The inhabitants of Manda defied the Portuguese, saying that only the sun and moon could effect an entrance into their invincible city, but when the Portuguese landed they ran into the bush, and the town was destroyed. It must have been rebuilt, as it is mentioned from time to time in the seventeenth century, and a sheikh of Manda was executed in 1678 as part of the programme of pacification carried out by Almeida. It was finally abandoned at the beginning of the nineteenth century as a result of lack of water.

The ruins consist of the remains of a large mosque, a smaller mosque with a trefoliate qibla, and some lengths of wall, including some with coral blocks, at the side of one of the creeks between which the town is built. An undated dedication inscription from the small mosque is in the Fort Jesus Museum. In 1953 a Mau Mau detention camp was set up near the site, and some imbecile warder and his equally imbecile wards extracted the stone, thinking that gold was hidden behind it. No excavations have yet been carried out at Manda, but it is unlikely that any of these buildings are older than the sixteenth or seventeenth century. The large mosque is on the edge of the bluff and might have been demolished by the Portuguese cannon during the bombardment of 1589.

The channel between Manda and Pate is enlivened from time to time by the appearance of a sea-monster of the conventional type with long neck and back. It apparently pops up every two or three years to see if anything has happened, satisfies itself that the state of the Lamu Archipelago is unchanged and goes down again. Manda Bay is a sheltered, wide and extremely deep anchorage. Unfortunately there is no inducement for anybody to use it, so the sea-monster is likely to be disappointed for many years.

Between the island of Manda and the mainland is a narrow mangrove-fringed channel called the *Mkanda*, which is only navigable at full tide during the neaps and half tide during the springs. The sea outside the island is rough and most travelling between them is done through the *Mkanda*. This insignificant stretch of water has the distinction of being mentioned in the *Periplus*. The *Mkanda* opens into Lamu Bay about half way between the jetty on the mainland at Mkowe and the town itself.

At the other end of the island, approached by a narrow winding creek from Lamu Bay, are the ruins of Takwa, a walled settlement of about five acres with a large mosque and out-buildings and some small houses. It was built on the slope of a hill going down to the creek and from the crest can be seen a line of sandhills and the breakers of the Indian

Ocean about a mile away. Excavations were carried out in 1950 and the settlement was seen to have been of short duration, possibly two hundred years between A.D. 1500 and 1700. Over the qibla of the mosque is a pillar, as on the small mosque at Shanga, and in the forecourt, incised in the plaster, some small drawings of dhows. In the cistern was found a seventeenth-century blue-and-white plate with a Maltese cross in the bottom, of Talavera ware.

By the creek is a tomb with a cylindrical pillar, crosses at each corner, and a tablet on the wall bearing an inscription "Abd Allah Muhammad Ali, al mutawaffa sana (who died in the year) 1094" (A.D. 1682). This tomb is, however, known by the name of Sheikh Fatihi Mansur, who was a disciple of Sheikh Abdalla, and is a place of annual pilgrimage for the people of Shela.

Takwa is not mentioned by the Portuguese, and only casually in the history of Pate as a town conquered by Sultan Omar. In the sixteenth century it would appear to have been the residence of a holy man and his disciples. Otherwise it is difficult to explain the size of the mosque and the scarcity of other buildings. It must always have been a difficult place to live in since there is little water.

At the south-east end of the island, at the mouth of the entrance to the harbour opposite Shela, is the site and fort of Kitau. Kitau was one of the towns destroyed by Pate in her period of aggression. Queen Mwana Inali is said to have thrown herself into the sea from Kitau Head when she heard her ministers had gone to Pate to surrender. In another version, for those progressive people who like common sense endings, she went to Pate and lived out her days in comfortable obscurity. There are no traces of any buildings or even mounds where Kitau is supposed to have been, except a few grave mounds which could be any date. The fort at Kitau is a nineteenth-century redoubt with its iron "broadsides" lying without their carriages in the embrasures.

Lamu is a sandy island which has flourished because of its position and, as important, its excellent water. It is the best port between Burkao and Mombasa and one of the few natural harbours on the coast of East Africa. No excavations have yet been carried out in the town or in the sandhills at each end, which are said to have been the sites of the two original settlements. According to tradition the settlement on the inward side called Weyuni was founded by Arabs from Yenbo in the Hedjaz; the other settlement on the seaward side called Hedabu, by Arabs from Oman, perhaps the brothers Suleiman and Said who fled from Oman in the seventh century. The Omani Arabs became the dominant power and Lamu flourished as a town of luxury and peace, generally as a satellite to Pate, but ready to surrender rather than suffer when trouble arrived.

In 1505 it quickly capitulated to the Portuguese and again in 1589. However, this easy surrender did not save its sheikh, who was executed at Pate for having handed over the ex-Captain of Malindi to the Turks. Another sheikh was executed in 1678, without any overt opposition. The quieter sultans of Pate preferred to marry and live at Lamu where life was less annoying or perilous. In the eighteenth century it showed a certain independence and even bellicosity, when it fought the Nabahani of Pate and the Mazrui of Mombasa. In 1812 it defeated them both with great slaughter at Shela, but this was its last battle. The people of Lamu realized that the virtues and the vices of peace were more in their line. They appealed to Seyyid Said, and in the year of the great victory the fort of Lamu was begun which was to be garrisoned by Omani soldiers.

Today Lamu is the most truly Arab town of the coast of East Africa. It is in fact the only town that has survived Somali, Portuguese, cannibals, Galla, British, and may even survive the Africans. It is the Bokhara of the coast, though now one reads that even Bokhara has accepted progress in the Russian manner. It produces nothing except a few coconuts, and its existence depends on the export of mangrove poles, coir fibre, simsim and dried fish, and the remittances of its Mombasa expatriates, not always very respectable people. Unregenerate, grasping, perverted, polite and profoundly suspicious—it is refreshing to find one place in the world that does not pretend to believe in progress or indeed in motion at all.

There are few recognizable old buildings in Lamu. The lower parts of the larger houses on the landward side of the main street and on the slope behind may go back several hundreds of years, and there may be cellars, once ground floor rooms, below them. It would be interesting to excavate one of the ruined houses to find the earliest level of occupation. Nothing has come to light accidentally which can be earlier than the thirteenth century. At the back of the town is a graceful fluted pillar rising from the façade of a partly buried tomb. In the sixteenth century the Dominican Friar João dos Santos described the people of Lamu as Shia, but now they are orthodox Sunni. The stricter Muslims say the pillar tombs are Shia and thoroughly disapprove of them. Once a year there is a popular festival of the Birthday of the Prophet, and the Maulid al Nebi at Lamu is the most famous and frequented of all. It is not very old and was founded by a sherif from the Hadhramaut in the middle of the last century. In the District Commissioner's residence is a brass horn "the *Siwa* of Lamu" which is said in the Khabar al Lamu to have been captured from the people of Mudiwo, perhaps Idio, near Mkanumbi on the mainland.

Lamu is about two miles from the open sea. At the entrance to the estuary is the village of Shela where live the descendants of the people who once inhabited Manda. The present buildings are of no great age, but from the sherds found on the beach, the site has been occupied for at least five hundred years. The ruined houses, which resemble those of Siyu, indicate that it was most prosperous in the middle of the nineteenth century. It is now a village of old men and young children; most adult males are working in Mombasa. A Portuguese chapel is mentioned but the building said to have been the chapel has now fallen into the sea.

4
The Tana Basin

THE MAINLAND behind the Bajun Islands is broken by wide creeks fringed with mangroves, but beyond the mangroves were agricultural settlements cultivated by the slaves of the *waungwana*, or free-born gentleman, who lived in Siyu or Pate. This country is now sparsely inhabited by ex-slave settlements and groups of Sanya, the hunting people of the coast akin to the Ata of Somalia. Many of them are relics of the dependent tribes of the Galla, who have remained after the annihilation of their masters by the Somali in the second half of the nineteenth century. On the other hand one group calling themselves Da'alo deny that they have anything to do with the other Sanya and are said to speak to each other in clicks. If this is true and they are really speaking, not just making encouraging noises, they are the aboriginal people of the Kenya coast and, according to some principles, should be its rightful owners. In actual fact, it would be extremely difficult to give it to them because their whole life is spent in flight, either from the Game Department who want them for poaching, or from the Administration who want them for Poll Tax.

In recent years the Giriama from beyond the Sabaki have begun infiltrating in search of good forest land owned by the state or absentee landlords. The abolition of slavery in 1897 had perhaps its most serious consequences in this area and many thousands of acres went out of cultivation. Neither landlord nor landless labourer had the intelligence to see

74

that a little generosity on the part of one and, equally if not more difficult, a little honesty on the part of the other would have enabled both to live well inside, instead of on the edge of subsistence. There are many parallels in the world around us, many affecting much larger and much more advanced communities than the bush landlords and labourers of Lamu.

There are no ruined towns until one reaches the long creek of Mkanumbi, which runs from opposite the south-west corner of Lamu island (see Fig. 4). Near the head of the creek and about one mile from it are the ruins of Luziwa, an old town said to have been once the home of the sheikhly family of Malindi. The unfortunate, retiring Portuguese Captain of Malindi, Relf de Brito, took refuge in Luziwa before going to Lamu, where he was handed over to the Turkish captain Mirale Bey. Later it paid tribute to Portugal as a minor state and is mentioned up till the end of the seventeenth century.

Today, in a dense patch of bush, are the remains of the town wall, some houses and a large mosque with a rather fine qibla. The present township of Mkanumbi on the main road, about half way between Witu and Lamu, has taken its place as the minor district centre.

Near the coast were a number of smaller settlements. Some of these are still occupied, such as Mea, Kiongwe and Kimbo; others, like Famau, are abandoned and lie nearly buried in sand dunes. At one time they belonged to the island towns, as for example, Mpekatoni to Lamu and Ukanga to Siyu. These two settlements were looted by the opposite parties in 1856 during the war between Seyyid Majid, Sultan of Zanzibar, and Muhammad Mataka, Sheikh of Siyu.

All this area is part of the prehistoric basin of the old Tana River, whose earlier courses can be seen from the air and which was once a much bigger river than it is today. In the sixteenth century it seems to have broken up into a number of streams, for it appears to be unknown to the Portuguese. As late as the middle of the nineteenth century it came out ten miles south of Kipini, and its present lower course was the independent Ozi River, draining the highland of Witu.

75

The construction of the Belazoni Canal between the two rivers in the eighties of the nineteenth century, by the Sultan of Witu, Ahmad Simba, in order to tax the produce going down to Kipini, caused it to change its course and it has never gone back. A number of schemes have been put forward for a greater utilization of the lower reaches of the Tana, but most of them have been shelved because of the possible consequences to the existing economy. In fact, there is no real reason why the Tana should take its present course more than any other, and when there are heavy rains the whole basin becomes a flooded plain with streams making themselves whenever there is the opportunity of uneven ground.

On the banks of the Tana live the Pokomo, a branch of the Nyika people with the same story of emigration from Shungwaya, but with the difference that they only ran as far as the Tana, where they settled and became a subject people to the conquering Galla. After the destruction of the Galla by the Somali in the eighteen sixties, they became subject to the Arabs and Swahili of Kau and Witu. They tend to be derided by the other Nyika peoples and stories are told of their general helplessness. On one occasion an earnest-minded District Commissioner tried to inspire them to cope with the baboon menace, which they complained was making their agriculture particularly unprofitable. The conversation went rather on these lines:

> D.C. "Why don't you make traps? Didn't your fathers make traps?"
> Pokomo. "If our fathers could have made traps, they would have made traps."
> D.C. "But you are more educated than your fathers. Have you not more intelligence?"
> Pokomo. "As regards intelligence, the baboons have us beat."

Even so, the Pokomo have survived in the malarious, flood-swept Tana basin and make quite a good living out of rice cultivation and bananas.

The Pokomo of the upper Tana are a different type, and on the whole have held their own against the Galla with some success. They differ physically from the Pokomo of the lower Tana owing to admixture with the Kamba, a Bantu tribe living on the western flank of the Nyika waste, which is now largely occupied by the Tsavo Royal National Park.

The Tana flows into Formosa or Ungwana Bay at the old District centre of Kipini, a decayed Swahili fishing village which at no distant date is likely to be washed away by the sea (Fig. 6). It was occupied in the nineties when a fort, which has now disappeared, was built in the course of the operations against Fumo Bakari, the Sultan of Witu. Later, when the Protectorate Administration was set up in 1895, Kipini was chosen as the district centre for the Tana River District. Although it was at the furthest end of the district, it was believed that it was the only place on the river where a European, who was not a missionary, could live. It is not clear whether missionaries were considered hardly European or under especial divine protection.

The District Commissioner's house was built in 1907. It is haunted by several independent ghosts who, in true British tradition, have not been introduced and therefore do not speak to each other. One is a European woman, the mother of an unfortunate young District Officer, who shot himself when delirious with malaria and suffering from an unsympathetic District Commissioner. As an ex-District Officer I know what he felt, but I was much more inclined to shoot my superior than myself. His mother was living with him at the time, and the poor woman is said to come into the house and tell the District Commissioner what she thinks of him. The other is an anonymous gentleman who rolls heavy objects, perhaps cannon balls, over the wooden floor: I have heard him frequently at his games. There is also a ghostly *safari* which assembles outside the house and then fades away in the blackness of the night.

A few yards from the main entrance is a small cemetery with three crosses; one belongs to the unfortunate young man just mentioned; the second to a District Commissioner who died from heat stroke on the river returning from *safari*. He was a Somerset Maugham character and the author of

the following poem which he left as his contribution to the
political records.

"Ship me somewhere East of Suez—"
The man who could write such rot
Should come and live
And the best years give
Of his life in this God-damned spot.

I'm sick of spicy breezes
I loathe your coral strand
And the surf that roars
On the reef girt shores
Of this God-forsaken land.

Old Mac the Government Doctor
Gave me at most a year:
There's nine months gone
And I still live on
If you call it living here.

I know my number's hoisted
I'm only skin and bone
But I shan't much grieve
For the life I leave
When I start for the great unknown.

Let us hope that his posting was not delayed.

The third grave holds the manager of a coconut estate, who
died of blackwater fever and of whom no story has survived.
There were once several graves, said to be of missionaries,
but they have disappeared; possibly they couldn't stand the
company. The station has now been closed and the District
Commissioner lives well up the river in the centre of his district. The house remains untenanted, a resthouse for the
rare visiting official. I wonder if the ghosts miss the company
of the living. Do they look forward, like old servants in a
country house, to the arrival of the master or even his guests,
ready to do each one his service?

About two miles east of Kipini are the ruins of the three
towns of Ungwana (probably the Hoja of the Portuguese),

Shaka also known as Paca, and Mwana (probably the Komwana of the Pate history).

Ungwana is the largest of the three and is one of the most impressive of the ruined towns of East Africa. The ruins cover an area of about fifty acres and include two Great Mosques, two or more smaller mosques—one with an elaborate qibla, which might have been a *chapelle royale*—a number of large houses, some fine tombs, and a town wall. It is built on a line of sandhills which are now about a quarter of a mile from the beach. Excavations were carried out in 1953 and 1954. The two Great Mosques, and the Mosque of the Domed Mihrab (the *chapelle royale*) were cleared; minor excavations were carried out around the tombs and at two places on the sea wall. The finds from the earliest levels were similar to the finds at other excavated sites, but in the fifteenth century they began to differ both in local earthenware and in some of the glazed wares from the Arab world. It would appear that the contention of the Sheikh of Malindi that the Tana basin had once been subject to him was correct. The difference in the imported wares shows that these African towns had varying trading connexions, and the presence of Egyptian wares recalls the statement of the Sheikh of Hoja to Tristan da Cunha, that he was the subject of the Soldan of Egypt. This is the only instance of any ruler on the coast claiming to be a subject of any external power.

The later Great Mosque built in the sixteenth century differed from the other Great Mosques of the coast in that it had two fine doorways, one on each side of the qibla, and a stone staircase minbar (Plate 7 and Fig. 1d). Stone minbars of this type are uncommon anywhere, and so far as I know this is the only one in East Africa. In the front of the qibla was found a fine crackled celadon bowl of the early fifteenth century, which had fallen out of its cavity and had lain broken and unwanted until it was covered with humus.

The other Great Mosque, which is adjacent to it, is rather a mystery. It had a small plain qibla but there was no sign of supports for the roof. On the west was an anteroom which had been roofed by cupolas and a barrel vault across the north

79

end where was the main entrance. In the debris of the fallen cupolas were found pieces of six celadon dishes of the late fourteenth or early fifteenth century.

A few hundred yards from the Great Mosque are the "Tombs of the Gentlemen". Ungwana is an abbreviation of the full place name which was Kiva N'Gwena Wamasha Shaka, meaning the Association of the Freeman of the Sheikhs of Shaka. Most of the tombs are the usual coastal type, open, rectangular enclosures with stepped corners and panelled sides. Two, however, are more elaborate, with rows of cavities for bowls and the stumps of fluted pillars. One of the two has panels decorated with a cross *fitché* diaper (Plate 8*a*). There are only two examples known to me of the use of this motif on a Muslim building, namely, on the façade of the Great Mosque of Veramin near Teheran built in 1334, and above the arches of the Great Mosque of Gulbarga in the Deccan, the first Bahmani capital built at the end of the fourteenth century. From the sherds of bowls found below the foundation level, these tombs cannot be earlier than the end of the fifteenth century.

The Mosque of the Domed Mihrab has an unusual mihrab or qibla. (The word mihrab is not normally used in East Africa or the Hadramaut, and in this case it is only used for euphony!) All qiblas I have seen in East Africa consist of an alcove squared on the outside and rounded inside over the roof, like a shell. But this qibla is an independent structure attached to the north wall, with a polygonal outside and a conical roof topped by an onion-shaped finial like a rococo pavilion; inside, it is rounded and fluted in the normal manner.

The bowls and inscriptions have been methodically removed from the tombs and mosques. It is possible that this deed was carried out by the French explorer M. Revoil who came down the coast in the eighties, or by a German Herr Tost, who was endeavouring to grow cotton here in the nineties. Rumour says Herr Tost was an officer in the Imperial Guard who had married a commoner and had to resign his commission. He lived in a house on the ridge behind Ungwana until the 1914 war when he was interned. When the war was

10. Vasco da Gama Pillar, Malindi. Late fifteenth century.

11(a) Tombstone of Sultan Omar bin Muhammad of Pate. Early fourteenth century.

(b) Tombstone of Mwana Majid binti Ma'adi bin Wabi al Kindiya, dated 1792.

over, there was no Kaiser and no Imperial Guard and he was able to return to Germany and live the life of a country gentleman with his "low-born" wife. If either of these gentlemen took the bowls and the inscriptions they may turn up one day in a continental museum, but so far I have been unable to find any trace of them.

Ungwana is supposed to be haunted, but there are so many ghosts of personality at Kipini that the shadowy wraiths of Ungwana can hardly compete. There are still some large animals in the bush among the ruins whose spoor I used to see in the morning when I was excavating. I have never seen a lion in the Great Mosque although I was told— afterwards I am glad to say—that a buffalo followed me when I was doing a reconnaissance of the town wall.

Ungwana is almost certainly the town of Hoja, which was stormed by Tristan da Cunha in 1505 at the request of the Sheikh of Malindi, who said that it had revolted against him. During the battle there was a charming, one might say "almost unique" instance of medieval chivalry which should not be forgotten. In the words of Captain John Stevens, who translated the "Portuguese Asia" of Faria y Sousa and dedicated it to Catherine of Bragança, the widow of Charles 11:

> George Silveyra, perceiving a grave Moor who led a Beautiful Young Woman through a Path in the Wood made at him, and the Moor making signs to the Woman to flee whilst they fought, she followed him, signifying she had rather die or be taken with him than escape alone, and Silveyra seeing them strive who should give the greatest demonstration of Love, let them both go saying God forbid my sword should part so much love.

The Sheikh of Hoja was killed outside the town in a desperate mêlée of swords and pikes in which I am sorry to say that the sentimental George Silveyra himself fell. Hoja was rebuilt and continued to be mentioned by the Portuguese until the end of the seventeenth century.

Four miles east of Ungwana on the shore itself are the ruins of Shaka, consisting of a mosque and a few houses of no great

F

interest. Shaka is associated with the story of Fumo Liongo, a mighty archer and a poet who was finally overcome by treachery—the usual fate of the technically invincible. Who he was and when he lived are obscure, but he would appear to have been a Swahili or Arab-African type who flourished at the end of the sixteenth century. An overgrown rectangular heap of stones, not far from the east wall of Ungwana, was pointed out to me as the grave of Liongo.

Another two miles along the shore are the more interesting ruins of Mwana. They include a fine Great Mosque with anterooms on both sides and another at the south end, and a small mosque with three aisles of four bays each, with a roof of cupolas and barrel vaults still in position. At Ras Mwana, which forms the northern limit of Formosa Bay, is a group of tombs of which the most striking has a carved coral boss with a cross *floré*, similar to the boss at Mnarani, surrounded by an illegible Arabic inscription. There is a story that these are the graves of seven virtuous maidens, the Mwana Mwali, who escaped the fate that is worse than death, how and when I have not discovered. Mwana can only be reached today by boat on a calm day or by walking along the beach when the tide is out, then walking back when the tide goes out again.

Not long ago the mouth of the Tana, the old Ozi, was six miles up the river near a site known as Kau, which is surrounded on one side by the Ozi and on the other by a creek called the Kirimanda. Kau also called Ozi was once the most important place on the river. It is first mentioned as the retreat of Ahmad bin Sheikh Fumoluti, an unsuccessful candidate for the throne of Pate. Driven from Pate by the Omanis he fled to Kau where in November 1824, with the consent of Captain Owen, he declared himself under a British protection. Later it became the headquarters of Ahmad Simba 1, who fled from Pate in 1856 after an unsuccessful campaign with Seyyid Said and set up a state in exile. He died at Kau and was succeeded by his nephew, also called Ahmad Simba. After an unsuccessful attempt on Pate he returned to the mainland, built a fort and a customs post, and laid dues on all river traffic like a robber baron on the Rhine. Later he moved to Witu where, no doubt, he felt healthier from a security as well as physical aspect. The fort at Kau has now disappeared but its outline, surrounded by a cemetery, can be traced. It is supposed to be haunted by the spirits of murdered Africans. Twenty miles up the river from Kau is the missionary station of Golbanti, one of the oldest in the country. It was founded by the Free Methodist Missionary Society in the eighties. In 1885 it was attacked by a Masai band and the missioner, Mr. Haughton, and his wife were speared. In 1895 it was attacked by Somalis, but the attack was beaten off. Further north was the German mission of Ngau, both are now managed by the Free Methodist Missionary Society.

Witu is built on a hill, about sixteen miles from the mouth of the Tana and ten miles from Kau. It is surrounded on the north and west by a patch of primaeval forest where there are still elephant and lion.

Witu made a brief appearance in history in the middle of the nineteenth century. In 1867 Sultan Ahmad, although he was almost always victorious in his battles with the troops of Seyyid Khalifa and Seyyid Barghash, signed a treaty with the German explorer Brenner by which his state was recognized as a German Protectorate. In 1888 he died and was succeeded by his cousin Fumo Bakari. The Protectorate apparently flourished and ten German expert advisors arrived to teach the Witu people to be better soldiers and better agriculturists, in the approved "big brother" manner.

In 1890 Germany surrendered her interest in the Protectorate of Witu, as part of the general settlement of the coast, but the Protectorate continued under Britain. Fumo Bakari becamed alarmed at the activities of his German friends and stopped them. On September 14, 1890 there was an altercation at the gate of Witu which was followed by a massacre of the Germans, not only those involved at Witu but also two others who were at Mkanumbi and nearby Hidiyo. Fumo Bakari refused to give satisfaction and a British expeditionary force landed at Kipini, defeated Fumo

Bakari in a midnight battle at Shaka la Simba, on the road between Kipini and Witu, and then stormed Witu and drove the Sultan into the bush where he carried on a guerilla war for some years until he died. He was succeeded by a half-witted brother, and then by another brother, Fumo Omari. Fumo Omari had ideas of reviving the glories of Ahmad Simba but he was unlucky or ill-judged in his efforts. First he tried to seduce Sir Arthur Hardings, Consul-General, Zanzibar, with the spectacle of his harem in various stages of undress. Then he tried to collect a stock of arms in the bush, but Captain Rogers—"our man at Witu"—had had enough of his nonsense and packed him off to Zanzibar, where he is said to have died of fright during the British bombardment of the Palace of Zanzibar in 1895. The Palace of the Sultan of Witu, such as it was, was destroyed in the storming of the town and the last relics of it, a fine pair of carved doors, were sold some years ago and are now in America.

The main road from Lamu and Witu going south crosses the Tana at Garsen, where the river is narrowest and there is a wire ferry. It then continues across a desolate and waterless stretch of country for about fifty miles, ten miles from the shore, until it reaches Gongoni where there is water and a turn off to the old site known today as Ngomeni (see Fig. 6).

The old Ngomeni is said to have been built on a sand bank on the north flank of Sheshale Point, between the sea and the salt water lagoons, but was almost completely washed away. Heavy rains up-country had filled the lagoons with the overflow waters of the Tana; an exceptionally high tide and strong easterly winds blew the waters of the sea against the land, and the fresh waters and salt met among the houses of the town. The cause of this misfortune is said to have been the extravagance of the women who used to bathe in goats' milk. I wonder what the chronicler of Ngomeni would have thought of all the natural aids to loveliness that are put out by the television screen today. He would have had no difficulty in explaining the natural calamities that even now occasionally make man, with all his mastery of nature, look uncommonly silly. All that remains of the old town are the ruins of a house on the headland near the present fishing village. The date of this remarkable event is uncertain but the *Kitab al Zenuj*, that mendacious document, relates that the people of Ozi came from Ngomeni. By Ozi could be meant Ungwana, which would put the inundation of Ngomeni sometime in the thirteenth century. The present inhabitants of Ngomeni are in no danger of succumbing to the temptations of their predecessors. Their last hopes foundered some years ago, when a boatload of poached ivory was captured by the Kenya Police Reserve as it coasted along the shore opposite Malindi on its way to a rendezvous with a dhow anchored in the old Malindi roads.

5

Malindi and the North Mainland

MALINDI, MELINDE, MA-LIN, is one of the oldest and most widely known place names in East Africa. It appears in a Chinese geography of the eleventh century; reference is made to it by the Arab-Sicilian Idrisi at the end of the twelfth, and it was one of the places mentioned as visited by the junks during the fifth Voyage of Cheng Ho, 1417–19. Unfortunately, there is considerable doubt as to whether the pleasant seaside resort of Malindi is the Malindi of all these stories.

The first is the most descriptive:

> South-west from Fu-lin (the Chinese name of the Roman orient), after one traverses the desert for two thousand miles is a country called Ma-lin. It is the old P'o-sa. Its people are black and their nature is fierce. The land is pestilentious and has no herbs, no trees and no cereals. They feed the horses on dried fish; the people eat *hu-mang*; the *hu-mang* is the Persian date. They are not ashamed of debauching the wives of their fathers or chiefs; they are (in this respect) the worst of the barbarians. They call this to seek out the proper master and subject. In the seventh moon they rest completely. They (then) do not send out nor receive (any merchandise) in trade and they sit drinking all night long.
> (*Duyvendak*).

The more lurid details may or may not be correct, but there are no dates today at Malindi.

Idrisi is more succinct. "Melinde a town at the mouth of a

FIG. 6. *The coast of Kenya*

river in the land of the Zinj". There is a river—the Quilimanci of the Portuguese, the Sabaki of today—but it is six
miles north of Malindi and is unlikely, I am informed, to
have come out anywhere else in historical times or at least
in the last thousand years.

The report of Cheng Ho is a bare mention of the name of the
town but, in the map which accompanies it, Malindi is put

87

in the latitude of Pangani. Old maps are not necessarily accurate, although in this case the northern part of the coast is shown in tolerably good proportion. On the popular, often fallacious belief that if one egg in a basket is good the others must also be good, the Malindi of Cheng Ho was somewhere near Pangani and cannot be the Malindi north of Mombasa. However, there can be no doubt that whatever Malindi the Chinese junks visited, it was in East Africa, and the reason for the visit was the principal recreational attraction of Africa, namely game; to be precise one species of game—the giraffe. The Chinese were fascinated, like many people, by the giraffe, not only because it is very long and very high and de Gaullish, but because they associated it with the unicorn. The unicorn was remarkable, unlike the inhabitants of Ma-lin, for the purity of its life, and also for the clear proof which its presence brought that the golden age had come. A unicorn would never come to any country that was not perfectly governed, therefore if it did arrive the country was perfectly governed, irrespective of what envious and badly informed people might say. No unicorns had been seen for centuries, and the descriptions of the last manifestation were rather vague and frequently conflicting; there was no reason why a giraffe could not be a unicorn. A previous expedition of Cheng Ho had gone to Bengal and on his staff was at least one literary minded opportunist. When he saw the giraffe that had been brought from Malindi as a wedding gift for the Sultan, he realized that this was a heaven-sent opportunity as well as a heaven-born animal. The giraffe-unicorn was taken off the Bengali barbarians, who were not so well informed as the Chinese on these matters and, in case it died on the way, another was ordered from Malindi. Both giraffes arrived safely, and the visit to Malindi in 1417 was to take back the envoys who had brought them.

How long the unicorn-giraffe lived is uncertain but there are numerous drawings, not at all convincing, of giraffes, but it would be improper to draw a heavenly animal with the veracity that the Chinese artists achieved with ordinary creatures. Giraffes are now recognized for what they are, and no longer mistaken for unicorns. There has been a great change in our views on such things. There has, however, been little change in the words considered suitable for these similar occasions. When the first unicorn arrived, the Board of Rites asked to be allowed to present a Memorial of Congratulation. The Emperor declined. "Let the Ministers early and late exert themselves in assisting the Government for the welfare of the world. If the world is at peace, even without K'i-lins, there is nothing that hinders good government". The orientals were as global minded in the fifteenth century as they are in the twentieth. When the second giraffe arrived, the same excellent form was maintained. "This event is due to the abundant virtue of the late Emperor my father, and also to the assistance rendered me by my ministers. That is why distant people arrive in uninterrupted succession. From now on it behoves you to remonstrate with us about our shortcomings". The sentiment was admirable. No British Prime Minister has done better. The last phrase of course was not meant to be taken literally; Chinese emperors had no more time than democratic politicians to heed time-wasting criticisms by out-of-date reactionaries.

Whatever reservations archaeologists may have about medieval Malindi, there is no doubt that the present Malindi is the Melinde of Vasco da Gama. The great Captain anchored off Malindi on April 13, 1498, and for the first time succeeded in making and maintaining amicable relations with the Sheikh and citizens of an East African town. Dr. Axelson, the historian of the Portuguese in East Africa, states a little harshly that he may have made fewer diplomatic mistakes at Malindi than anywhere else. This may be so, but errors in diplomacy and acts of brutality apart, the interests and principles of the Portuguese and the Arabs were so contrary that they could not be reconciled. As in the past the Arabs are believed to have driven the Indonesians off the seas, so the Portuguese were to destroy the Arab monopoly of the Indian Ocean, and then to be reduced themselves to impotence by the Dutch. Malindi was the favoured town of the coast, but the favours she received were not uninterrupted and one is frequently reminded of the treatment of subject allies by the Romans in the past, the Nazis of yesterday and the Russians of today and tomorrow. The Malindi of those days was a small oriental town with whitewashed single-or double-storied houses and narrow streets, not unlike Lamu today, built on the sandhills and coral outcrops around the present water tower. The shore line has altered considerably. The foundation trenches of the Malindi Bar near the jetty produced no porcelain earlier than the fifteenth century, and the road along the seafront to Silversands is laid on land which has comparatively recently been released by the sea. Malindi was surrounded by a town wall, but there were many gardens and houses outside the walls. Some sherds of four-teenth-century pottery came from the site of houses beyond the lighthouse, and fourteenth- or fifteenth-century porcelain came from a building under the Sindbad Hotel.

The two remarkable Pillar Tombs in front of the attractive modern mosque were ornamented with fifteenth-century celadon bowls (Plate 9a). The large tomb inside the enclosure of the larger pillar tomb is late fifteenth century. These tombs must have been standing when the Portuguese arrived but, curiously enough, are never mentioned by them. The pillars are two of the finest surviving examples of this type of monument, and are said, sometimes with embarrassing familiarity, to be obviously phallic.

Pillar Tombs are the one architectural invention of the coast of East Africa. They are supposed to represent the male organ and they may be connected with the phallic pillars of the Galla or the monolithic pillars of the Imerina and Betsileo of Madagascar, which have a similar significance. They are considered by the orthodox Muslims to be Shia, and if so, they may be a legacy of the lost Almozaid. The Almozaid are stated by the Portuguese historian de Barros to have been the earliest Arab settlers: "From their entrance, like a slow plague, they spread along the coast". They were the followers of Zaid, the grandson of Hussein, who had fled from perse-cution in Arabia in the seventh century. They founded the first settlements but were evicted by fresh waves of Arabs who were orthodox Sunni. "They withdrew into the interior, intermarried with the cafres and adopted their customs in such a manner that they became half-breeds in every way". "Withdrew into the interior" probably meant they moved further south along the coast. It is uncertain what Barros meant by "halfbreeds in every way" but he was certainly not being complimentary. "These are the people whom the Moors living on the coast called Baduiis." The Bajuns of today are merely a fisher and mangrove cutting people and building in stone is quite unfamiliar to them. The adoption of pillar tombs may have been part of the Africanization or de-Arabization. If your own people have been beastly to you it is easy to adopt foreign customs, however repugnant they may have been to you when you first met them.

The earliest pillar tomb investigated is that on the island of Kilepwa, which may be fourteenth century. They were still being erected in Tanganyika in the nineteenth century, but have now gone out of fashion. The earliest typologically would be the circular pillars. The Kilepwa pillar is octagonal; the three at Gedi are fluted, octagonal and hexagonal; in Tanganyika and Pemba square pillars are preferred. It would seem that the people who were erecting them had forgotten what they were trying to do, as, not only are they highly schematized but they are not even consistent in their schematization. In fact any form of pillar was acceptable.

The palace of the Sheikh of Malindi is said to have been on the shore and the Sheikh to have come down a flight of steps to welcome Vasco da Gama. The site would appear to be either on the hill near the tombs or just beyond above the jetty. No important foundations have been uncovered on either site and there is no real evidence of identification. The broken-down mosque and tombs in the fishing village are also fifteenth century. Otherwise nothing of the Arab past has survived.

At the end of the rocky promontory on the south side of the town is the cross or padrão of Vasco da Gama one of the most remarkable survivals of time (Plate 10). It is of Lisbon limestone, bears the coat-of-arms of Portugal and was

brought by the great Captain. It was set up originally outside the Sheikh's house. It was then taken down, in view of the
odium it excited, but was re-erected after the Portuguese
had made Malindi their northern headquarters in 1512 and
were in a position to protect their friends. It is not mentioned
by the Portuguese travellers of the middle of the sixteenth
century and may have fallen down, but was re-erected with
its cone-shaped support sometime before the Portuguese
moved to Mombasa in 1593.

The Portuguese settlement at Malindi was at the south end
of the town, and the south-east corner of the small building
in the old Christian cemetery is part of the original Portuguese chapel. Traces of a Crucifixion were visible until some
years ago, when it was covered by whitewash. It is now
admirably preserved but will require the services of a specialist
to restore it to visibility. In this cemetery St. Francis Xavier
is believed to have buried several sailors on his way to India
in March 1542. He was engaged in polite conversion by some
pious Muslims. When they deplored, as one professional
man to another, the decline in faith, their ardent colleague
rounded on them and said he was surprised in view of the
doctrines they taught that they had followers at all. I do not
think Francis Xavier was a good conference type; in fact, I
do not think he ever got the idea of trying to get together
with those who held different views as to man's place and
destiny on earth. The United Nations would have been
utterly incomprehensible to him, as incomprehensible as the
idea that moral judgements should be affected by the shadow
of the atomic bomb or any other abnormal unpleasantness.

Malindi prospered throughout the sixteenth century with
the Portuguese patronage and the eclipse of her old rival
Mombasa. Visitors on their way to India commented on
the abundance and cheapness of the food, and the friend-
liness of the Sheikh and the inhabitants.

In 1586 on the occasion of the first sortie of the Turkish
fleet of Mirale Bey, it became the refuge of all Portuguese
on the coast. The new Portuguese Captain, Ruy Lapez
Salgado, was accused of pusillanimity, but it is difficult to

see what he could have done with the whole coast in revolt against him. On Mirale Bey's second sortie in 1589 he had to face the redoubtable Mateus de Vasconcelos. The Turkish galleys had reached Malindi in the evening and anchored for the night, intending to storm the town next morning. But Vasconcelos, knowing that in weakness the only hope is attack, set up two small cannon or falconets on a sandbank and fired on the Turkish ships throughout the night with such effect that at daybreak they pulled up their anchors and sailed on to Mombasa.

The next year Malindi was in graver peril. The horde of cannibals, known as the Zimba, who had eaten Kilwa in 1586 and Mombasa in 1589, were camped outside Malindi. Fortunately Vasconcellos had returned from the victorious expedition to Mombasa and organized the defence with customary efficiency. As the cannibals swarmed over the walls of the town and the adjacent Portuguese settlement, they were attacked in the rear by the Segeju, a mixed Bantu-Galla tribe whom he had paid to help him. The Zimba were cut to pieces and only a hundred with their leader are said to have returned to their starting point on the Zambezi through the lands they had devastated.

However, the golden age of Malindi was coming to an end. Early in 1593, the Sheikh became Sultan of Malindi and Mombasa and moved with the Portuguese to Mombasa. Without Sheikh or Portuguese, Malindi sank rapidly. In 1636 it is described in the profit and loss account of the Portuguese eastern possessions, called the *Livro do Estado do India Oriental* written in 1636 for the Viceroy, the Count of Linhares, as a place of small account and a liability.

The Kingdom of Melinde which is eighteen leagues to the north of Mombasa is a town on the mainland. Formerly it was no more than a small settlement of Moors. It is now decreased to a third part of the size it was. The Viceroy appointed as Governor a trusty Moor called Barcairanda, and ordered him to be given twenty-five scores of linen cloth and two candils of iron to disburse to the Mossegejos Caffres who continued to infest them. There is nothing else of interest in the Kingdom except the expenditure above-mentioned.

(Gray).

So much for the great city of Melinde of the early Portuguese pioneers. When Milton mentioned Kilwa and Malindi, Kilwa was in ruins and Malindi was on the way out. *Sic transit gloria mundi.* At the end of the seventeenth century the Sheikh and most of the Arabs were living in Mombasa. In 1823 the walls and deserted houses and the Vasco da Gama memorial were seen by Captain Owen in the course of his survey of the coast. He did not enter the harbour but anchored in Malindi Roads about six miles south-west where there is deep water. Malindi is ignored in the detailed account of the coast by Admiral Guillain made in 1846, and only briefly mentioned by Burton in 1854. It was reoccupied about 1854, by orders of the Sultan of Zanzibar, and was visited by Sir John Kirk in 1884. He mentions town walls and Portuguese tombstones, but they have since disappeared. At the north end of Malindi in a private garden are the remains of a small mosque with a trefoliate qibla, known as the Jemadari Mosque, which belongs to this period. The oldest of the present buildings dates from the last two decades of the nineteenth century, when the Imperial East Africa Company had a representative at Malindi who, after the proclamation of the Protectorate, became the District Commissioner. The present District Office is shown in a photograph in Fitzgerald's Travels in British East Africa, taken in 1896. The development of Malindi dates from the end of the last war when it began to be increasingly popular with up-country European settlers who said they liked to come down once a year to "sea-level and sanity".

Six miles north of Malindi the River Sabaki flows into the sea. The Sabaki, called the Galana in its middle reaches, rises in the Athi Hills south of Nairobi but draws much of its water from the Tsavo, which flows into it during flood times. The river is navigable in a sporting rather than practical sense. In 1505 an adventurous Portuguese called George Alfonso went up the river, then known as the Quilimanci,

94

for six days and saw a large number of hippopotamus. He was unable to make contact with the natives and running short of food he had to come back to Malindi. The river is shallow at low water and it is possible to walk across it.

Apart from their use as a means of portage, rivers have also served as tracks and in waterless country as a running water supply. An interesting story is told by the Portuguese writer de Barros in the same passage in which the journey of George Alfonso is described. Fifty years before a large party of natives had come down the river with gold to sell. After some days of negotiation the Sheikh of Malindi had taken it off them—so they not unnaturally never came back.

Two miles north of the mouth of the river is the small settlement of Mambrui, the Quilimanci of the Portuguese. Apart from some walls near the shore, the only remains of the past are the ruins of a large pillar tomb. The tomb collapsed about twenty years ago, but the top, with its frieze of the late sixteenth-century Ming porcelain bowls, remained intact (Plate 8b). The pillar stood about twenty-seven feet high and has a diameter of five and a quarter feet. It must have been one of the largest on the coast. It is marked on the Dalrymple charts, presumably as a navigation aid for ships coming from India which had been blown out of their course. The north-east coast of East Africa was seldom visited during the eighteenth century by European ships.

Mambrui today is a small township, living on the rich cotton-growing area on the left bank of the Sabaki. It is a centre of the old Arab life of the coast and its Maulid is second only to Lamu. South of Malindi, the coast line is broken by the large basin known as Mida Creek, the long inlet of Kilifi, and the lesser inlets of Takaungu or Kivuma and Shimo la Tewa. Near Mida is the town of Gedi, and the smaller settlements of Watamu, Kilepwa and Shaka. Gedi, where extensive excavations have been carried out, is the subject of a separate chapter. The beach bungalow settlement of Watamu is on the site of the small haven known to the Portuguese as Outamo. The large tomb on the beach was adorned with a very early blue-and-white plate and, with the little

95

mosque attached to it, may be fourteenth century. Kilepwa is a settlement on an island commanding the entrance to the inner anchorage of Mida Creek. There are the ruins of a small mosque, a group of large houses and an elaborate pillar tomb. Excavations were carried out in 1950 and below the ruins were found early *sgraffiato* and local earthenware. It was abandoned at the same time as Gedi. The word means "the place that dried up", which shows that there was a time when there was more sub-surface water than there is today.

Kilifi was a more important town. It is mentioned frequently by the Portuguese. The centre seems to have been a walled settlement on a bluff on the south side of the creek, now known as Mnarani. The ruins today consist of a fine group of tombs including one pillar tomb (Plate 9*b*) and two mosques (Fig. 1*c*). Among the collapsed tombs destroyed by falling trees a large number of broken funeral inscriptions were found. In fact, there is a greater footage of old Arabic at Mnarani than any other site in East Africa, except Mogadishu. The inscriptions are written in an extremely difficult form of monumental Arabic which, so far, has not found an interpreter. The experts say they are very hard to read, very badly cut, mean nothing and would take more time to work out than is available. Four good, if somewhat inconsistent, reasons for doing nothing. It is, generally speaking, more difficult to persuade an epigraphist to read an inscription than it is to seduce a virtuous woman. However, it is hoped that this will not always be the case, or at least that some epigraphist will make a study of East Coast inscriptions.

The mosque was one of the most elaborate in East Africa. In the spandrels of the arch of the qibla were carved coral bosses, one with a cross *floré*. On both sides were large Arabic inscriptions with letters eighteen inches high. Unfortunately, the mosque has suffered from bush fires and these magnificent examples of decorative Arabic have almost vanished. The north-east entrance of the mosque had also been burnt, which would appear to be corroboration of the story that Kilifi was stormed by the Galla. The unfortunate inhabitants had locked themselves in the mosque hoping for the help that never came. Kilifi is mentioned in 1618, and the usual late sixteenth- or early seventeenth-century sherds of porcelain were found, so this event would have occurred in the second quarter of the seventeenth century. In the cistern of the small mosque was found a blue-and-white plate, with a white earthenware body and an imitation Chinese design, which is Portuguese Delft. Three miles away on the north side of Takaungu Creek is a small settlement of the same date, known as Kitoka. These two settlements and a third on the site of the present district centre of Kilifi made up the old state of Kilifi, which was acquired with Mombasa by the Sheikh of Malindi after the victorious campaigns of his Segeju allies in 1589. Fugitives from Kilifi make up one of the Nine Tribes of Mombasa.

South of Kilifi along the coast to Mombasa there is a string of settlements which are represented by ruins of mosques and tombs. An interesting group of pillar tombs, probably sixteenth century, is to be found at Kurwitu, half way between Kilifi and Mtwapa. This would appear to have been an Arab manor or villa which had been occupied for two or three generations and then abandoned after the Galla had taken Kilifi. The area is honeycombed with large coral caves or grottos which, from the quantities of broken pots found in them, must have been inhabited for a time, probably in the nineteenth century, perhaps by slaves awaiting shipment. There are other scattered settlements including two of some size: Mtwana la Jumbe and Mtwapa, the latter on the north bank of an inlet similar to Kilifi but not as wide. No excavations have been undertaken but sherds of the fourteenth and fifteenth centuries have been found at both sites. Mtwana la Jumbe appears to have been the larger of the two. There are the remains of two mosques, one quite large, a pillar tomb and a curious circular walled structure like a miniature amphitheatre.

Mtwapa possesses a ruined mosque and the remains of a number of houses, including a storied building. The settlement is mentioned with Tuaca (Kilindini) by the Portu-

G

guese as an entrepôt for ivory, tobacco and opium, and it would have served as an outlet for the produce of the Chonyi hills. It was probably from here that the "King" of Chonyi sent supplies to Fort Jesus during the great siege. It was outside the region occupied by the Galla but, according to a tradition, it perished in the middle of the nineteenth century through civil war—the old story of an unexpected or privately expected visitor and a jealous husband. It is mentioned as the home of Khamis bin Kombo, the Temam or Sheikh of the Nine Tribes of Mombasa, who in 1895 took a prominent part in the last Mazrui rebellion and as a result was locked up in Fort Jesus. South of Shimo la Tewa Creek there is a series of beaches: Shanzu (the Sanxo of the Portuguese), Bamburi and Nyali, before the coast bends back to form the wide bay in which is set the island of Mombasa. On the north side of the bay is the site of the "Turkish Battery", referring to a position set up at the time of the second Turkish raid. The exact site has not been identified but it was probably Mackenzie Point opposite Fort Jesus. It was used during the unsuccessful attempt of Francesco de Moura to take the Fort in 1632. Cannon were again mounted here during the great siege, but it was too far from the Fort to do any damage and its sole use would have been to defend the entrance to Mombasa harbour.

6

Gedi

SIXTY-FIVE miles north of Mombasa and ten miles south of Malindi are the ruins of an Arab colonial town, known as Gedi. It was visited by Sir John Kirk in 1884 but was then forgotten for fifty years until, in 1927, it was gazetted an Historical Monument. It received a few desultory visitors, some of whom extracted the surviving bowls from the mosques and tombs to provide a little exotic interest to their humdrum homes. In 1939 valuable work was done by the ever-maligned Public Works Department of the Kenya Government in cementing together the crumbling walls of the more important buildings, such as the Great Mosque and the Tombs. Without this work there would have been very little standing when funds were made available for excavations. In 1948 Gedi was declared a National Park and an archaeologist was appointed to investigate it.

By then it was once more overgrown and before excavation could be started it was necessary to clear the bush, make paths and cut down a number of trees which threatened the buildings or obstructed the work. The trees were lopped and if possible cut down in pieces, using another tree as a "mast" to which the branch or limb to be cut could be attached. When this was not possible, it was sawn through near the base, and then pulled down where there was a gap between walls. Usually it was possible to find a position where there was six foot clearance and a good tug brought it straight down without damage.

Some of the walls had to be brought back to vertical or taken down and rebuilt. I was fortunate to have the services of an able and fearless Italian mason whose natural intelligence had not been destroyed by anything he had learnt at school. His greatest achievement was the restoration to vertical of the rear wall of the Great Mosque, which was in one piece but leaning outwards at a dangerous angle. It had been built partly on top of an older wall and partly over the floor, so it was in fact locked in position by the roof. However, with the disappearance of the roof it was free to follow its natural inclination, which was to fall outwards. Trees were cut down and laid as props against the inner and outer faces of the wall. A long tree was laid across the outer row as a cross beam, and movement was given to the installation by a one-ton block-and-tackle attached to another tree and bearing on the cross beam. The block was wound up, and the whole wall thirty feet long and ten feet high tottered backwards, to be held by the props on the other side.

The excavations at Gedi were mainly directed to the investigation of the history of the various buildings, and produced no great thrills. The average depth of occupation after surface clearance, sometimes quite considerable, was seldom more than six feet before natural coral was reached. In the houses there was usually an earlier floor, sometimes two, and sub-structural occupation. The rooms were usually empty and most of the finds came from fill levels or rubbish heaps.

The Giriama, the local African tribe, have shown themselves apt excavators. Apart from university students or the girls from Kensington Gore, I could not ask for better collaborators. They learnt at once the basic principles of digging in levels, and the importance of noticing changes of soil, and keeping the finds from different types of soil apart. They also appreciated the difference between the economics of archaeology and agriculture. In archaeology you are paid at the end of the month, whatever the success of the expedition; in agriculture you may get some money at the end of several months, if all conditions have been propitious, but by that time you have accumulated so many liabilities that you see

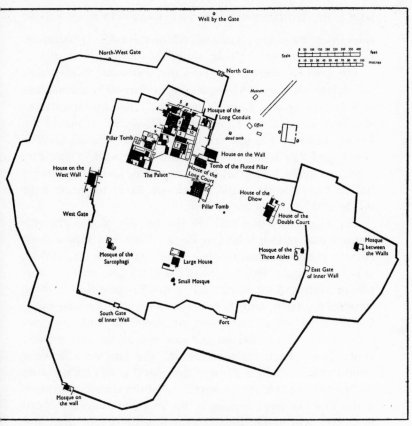

FIG. 7. *The Arab city of Gedi*
Key to numbered buildings

1. *House of the Cistern;*
2. *House of the Panelled Walls;*
3. *House of the Sunken Court;*
4. *House of the Venetion Bead;*
5. *House of Iron Lamp;*
6. *House of the Ivory Box;*
7. *House of the Cowries;*
8. *House of the Scissors;*
9. *House of the Chinese Cash;*
10. *Market.*

very little of it. I have never had any difficulty in getting willing and frequently interested labour.

The whole area was planned and the main buildings plotted. The outer wall encloses an area of about forty-five acres. Within is a Palace, a Great Mosque, seven private houses and three pillar tombs. The trace of the wall on the south and east follows the line of a prehistoric coral ridge standing about fifty feet above the present sea level. On the sides where there are no natural features, it takes an arbitrary line determined by the holdings of the original occupants.

The area excavated comprises the north-west corner with the Palace, the Great Mosque, and the largest concentration of surviving houses. Outside this area a few buildings have also been cleared: the House of the Dhow, the House of the Double Court, the South-east Gate on the inner wall, and the North and North-east Gates on the outer wall. There are, however, many areas still to be explored, including a large building outside the walls, which are likely to throw light on the vicissitudes of life at Gedi.

The Great Mosque built in the middle of the fifteenth century and rebuilt a hundred years later, is a typical East African congregational mosque or jumaa (Plate 12a and b). It is a rectangular building, with the qibla showing the direction of Mecca in the north wall, a minbar or pulpit of three steps on the right, and three doors in each of the long walls. On the west was an anteroom, subsequently converted into an open platform, and on the east a veranda and a court containing a well, conduit, cistern, and lavatory. Between cistern and veranda is a row of four coral bosses for scraping the soles of the feet. At the north end of the veranda is a store and a flight of steps leading to the roof from which the call to prayer was given. Owing probably to Ibadhi prejudice there are few old minarets in East Africa. The Ibadhis were the "Levellers" of Islam and believed that no man should stand above his fellows. However, to give the call to prayer from the ground was so inefficient because nobody could hear it, they had to make arrangements for the Mueddhin to go on to the roof of the mosque. Nevertheless, to recognize this objectionable necessity by building a minaret would have been unthinkable.

The Mosque was covered by a roof of coral tiles set in lime concrete, similar to the fragments lying on the east veranda. It was carried on square rafters supported on three rows of six rectangular pillars, the middle row running down the centre of the mosque. This is a maladroit arrangement found in many mosques in East Africa for which I can think of no explanation. Accepting the necessity for aisles of equal width, it would have been simple to have had two or four rows of pillars which would have left the qibla, the principal feature of the mosque, unobscured. The rear three bays are cut off by a wall from the main part of the mosque. This space may have been reserved for the use of women, or the wall may have been built to reduce the size of the mosque when the roof collapsed and the community could afford only a temporary roof over the forepart of the building.

Around the walls are pilasters with square niches for the boat-shaped oil lamps with which the mosque was illuminated during the hours of night prayers. The qibla consists of an alcove, with a pointed and stilted arch set in a square frame with a herring-bone border, once ornamented with porcelain bowls. In the spandrel of the north-east doorway is carved a broad-bladed spearhead. This is evidence of the mixed character of the ruling class of Gedi. No pure Arab would put a spearhead, which is a symbol of power and might, at the entrance of a mosque, a place to be entered in a spirit of humility. On the other side is said to have been a shield, but this was not found when the doorway was cleared.

The plan of the mosque and the court belongs to the original building but the mosque itself was rebuilt in the sixteenth century. Below the rectangular pillars can be seen the square pillars by which the roof was originally. supported. When the mosque was rebuilt the pillars were enlarged, thereby reducing the width of the aisles from eight to seven feet, rather suggesting that the mosque fell down and expert opinion considered that eight feet was too much for the weight of the roof. Fragments of the herring-bone ornament of the frame of the qibla were found beneath the floor in front of it, showing that the original qibla was taken to pieces and put together again when the mosque was rebuilt.

On the floor of the mosque was found a flask in a fine polished red earthenware with incised ornament of bulrush millet. This ware was made in India and is a distant relative of the famous Samian ware, the mark of Rome in western Europe. Around the well were found quantities of glass and shell beads. The women bend over and break their beads in drawing water and the archaeologist comes along a few hundred years later and picks them up.

The well, like almost all the wells of Gedi, was empty with only a few sherds and the stones of the wall that went across it in the bottom. The fact that none of the large wells of Gedi has been used as a rubbish pit shows that the town was abandoned at the time or soon after they had gone dry.

Near the mosque is the Tomb of the Fluted Pillar which is one of the oldest monuments at Gedi and probably ante-dates the Town Wall. The walls of the tomb behind it are not at right-angles to the façade of the pillar and they may belong to a later burial. To build a good tomb does not mean you will necessarily have it to yourself for eternity.

The Palace stands a few hundred yards from the Great Mosque, and with its Annexe, separated from it by a street, covers an area of about a quarter of an acre (Plate 13a and b, and Fig. 8). The main entrance is through a pointed arch on a platform approached by a flight of steps with a bench on each side. Beyond the arch another flight of steps leads down to a sunken court with benches on the two long sides. Sunken courts are a feature of the domestic quarters at Gedi. They served as reception rooms where the master of the house could meet his friends without having to admit them to his house. The oriental custom of seclusion of women raised problems for the architect as well as for everybody else. A room that was "of" the house but not "in" the house was a convenient solution when you wished to talk scandal or sedition. The purpose of the sunken court was to raise the relative height of the surrounding wall so as to ensure a longer shadow. In the reception court of the Palace, it was possible to be pleasantly in the shade on one or the other side of the court at any time in the day except between twelve and two. In the floor of the court are two sumps for rainwater. These revetted pits, about seventeen feet deep and three feet wide, are found in all the streets and courts of the town, and were designed to carry off the surface water which would otherwise have undermined the walls of the houses. To the left of the reception court is a large well and an open court with a sump in the middle of it. The hole in the sump was larger than the normal hole, and this court was probably used for washing clothes.

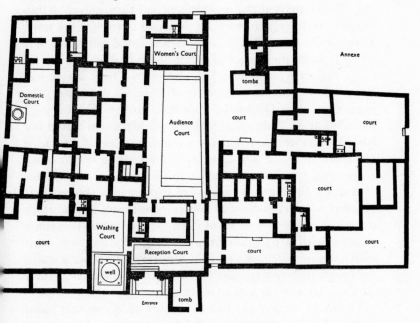

FIG. 8. *Plan of the Palace at Gedi*

A passage leads from the reception court to the audience court of the Palace. This consists of a rectangular court running in front of the main block of the Palace with platforms on east, south, and west sides. Originally there was a flight of steps in the middle of the platform on the residential side. This was covered up when the Palace was extended and the platform was widened and raised. In its final state, as is seen today, there was a bench along the east end where the sheikh or judges would sit, protected from the sun until mid-day by the wall behind them. The suitors in the court and their advocates would stand in the sun, so the proceedings would be kept short. A lawyer at Gedi would have had to have the skin of a salamander as well as the hide of an ox.

To be long in memory and wind would not have been sufficient.

One is reminded of Ibn Batuta's description of the court of the Sheikh of Mogadishu in the early fourteenth century. The Sheikh opened the proceedings and then retired, handing over to the Qadhi and the principal officers of the state. If any problem arose which the judges could not solve, they wrote it down on a piece of paper and sent it in to him. He never deferred judgement but always sent back an answer forthwith, sometimes possibly in diplomatic obscurity. The judges' bench at Gedi would not hold all the "High Gang" recorded at Mogadishu. It was a small place and would not have had more than a modest number of *sherif* and high officials. The room and lavatory behind would be the office accommodation for the Sheikh to give a private audience or wait for those annoying slips of paper which showed that his officers were reluctant to take responsibility. The lavatory is typical of the lavatories of Gedi. It consists of two small cubicles with a partition between them. In one was a pit with a square hole and a urinal channel; in the other a washing bench with two cavities for bowls in an upper tier and a divided seat, used as a bidet, in the lower.

The main block of the Palace is made up of an outer room with two pairs of rooms behind it. The outer room has a cupboard and niches in the pilasters framing the doors leading to the inner rooms. In the walls are rows of pegs for hanging carpets. The doorways have the characteristic pointed arches, no keystones, but two vertical stones over the apex. Between the two rear rooms is a chamber without a door. This was the strong room for storing valuables and the bags of cowries which were perhaps the currency of the coast. The rate is stated to have been 400,000 cowries to the gold dinar, though I rather feel that 40,000 is a more likely figure. The store would be entered by a small trapdoor high up in the wall, approached by a ladder. One or two of these stores with access from one of the bedrooms are found in every house. All were empty, which is evidence that Gedi was evacuated rather than stormed.

The main block of the Palace is in itself a typical Gedi house, but in this case it serves as the anteroom for the two wings, one possibly for staff and storage, the other for women, since it leads down to another reception court. This is one of the most interesting rooms in the Palace. It is entered at one end over a *fingo* or spell, which consisted of a pot containing a piece of paper with words written on it which was buried in the floor with appropriate incantations and by which it was believed that a djinn had been induced to take up residence in the pot. If anybody came in with evil intentions he would be driven out of his mind. The pot was buried near the door so that the miscreant would not have an opportunity to do very much before the djinn got him. Once a week incense was burnt over the pot, just to remind the djinn that he was there for a purpose. Two other pots have been found in similar positions at Gedi, one in the north-east gate, presumably aimed against political undesirables. On two sides of the room are benches and built into the wall in the south-east corner was a large jar which was used for storing beads. In the bottom was found a cornelian bead which had been cross-bored so it could not be threaded. One can imagine the hennaed fingers picking it out and throwing it back, and the inane conversion that followed. In the north wall was a small door where pedlars could sell their wares, but this had been blocked. It is possible that the pedlars were not always pedlars and they sometimes offered more interesting wares than cloth and beads.

The women's court is cut off by a blank wall from the audience court of the Palace, and the pedlar's door and the public entrance to the audience court are side by side. Opposite these doors is a group of tombs, including a tomb with a hexagonal pillar which is one of the best preserved on the coast. There is no epitaph and nothing except its propinquity to the Palace to suggest who was buried in it. He would have been a holy man, probably a *sherif*, and related to the ruling family of Malindi. There was a second and earlier pillar tomb behind it but this has collapsed.

Opposite the tombs is a building of three courts and four

apartments, each consisting of outer room, inner room and lavatory. One of the apartments faces the tomb and has an open veranda with a small room at the side. This could never have been used for normal domestic life and has the form of an oriental shop in which the goods would be displayed during the day on the veranda and locked away in the side room at night.

The East African rulers were not comparable in dignity with their contemporaries in Persia or India and they could only continue as monarchs so long as they were successful merchants. It is possible that this was the place where most of the porcelain found at Gedi was bought. The other apartments may have been harem or staff quarters. A *mziga* or horned bowl was found in one room; all the other rooms were empty. At the back of the rear court were two ancillary rooms which may have served as servants' quarters. At the end they had fallen into disuse and the doorway into them had been blocked.

The story of the Palace would appear to be as follows. A building consisting of the earlier audience court, the main block and the west wing or women's quarters was constructed in the early fifteenth century. In the second half of the century it was extended and the Annexe was built. At the beginning of the sixteenth century it was abandoned, but at the end of the century a large programme of renovation and tenementization was undertaken which was never completed.

Fourteen large houses in recognizable condition have been cleared, ten of them in the main excavated areas. They have been named after an architectural feature or the most interesting find in them. The majority are semi-detached, but unlike a semi-detached house of today the front doors are not side by side, so you do not have to know what your neighbour is doing. Of course you did, or your wife did, but it was not forced on your notice. The oldest surviving house in its original state is the House of the Cowries, built at the end of the fourteenth century. Some of the others are probably not much later but have been modified in the course of the fifteenth or at the end of the sixteenth century. Two of the latest are the House of the Scissors and the House of the Cistern in its present state.

The original house style, represented only by the House of the Cowries, consisted of a long narrow court in front, a long room with lavatory at the end, a second long room, and three smaller rooms at the back (bedroom, kitchen, and store). Subsequently the plan was changed by dividing the middle long room into two and making a house of one long room and two suites of two rooms each, presumably for the two wives with whom the master was living at the time. The kitchen was either omitted or formed part of a domestic court to which access was provided from the outside and also from one of the two suites. The shape of the front court was changed from a narrow rectangle suitable only for social life to a wide rectangle which could have had a commercial or industrial use. In the later houses also, as in the House of the Porcelain Bowl and the House of the Scissors, the lavatory was no longer part of the main block but was pushed out into the courtyard. A lavatory in the House of the Double Court was excavated and was found to be twenty-seven feet deep. It is possible that later lavatories were not built so efficiently.

The roofs of the houses were flat and carried on mangrove poles which had been squared by the adze. The use of mangrove poles explains why the rooms were long and narrow— there is no span greater than eight feet. It would have been difficult to get a large supply of longer poles which could be squared to produce rafters that could carry fifteen inches of lime concrete. The outer room generally had a ceiling of tiles under the mortar which was omitted in the middle rooms. The rear rooms or bedrooms generally had roofs of stamped red earth. The absence of windows and the thickness of roof and walls must have kept the houses pleasantly cool during the day. The relative gloom would not have mattered because nobody read for pleasure and nobody worried about the eyes of the women who did the sewing.

The household utensils can be seen in the Information Room. The kitchen ware and the eating bowls of the slaves were of local earthenware: cooking pots, jars, lamps, eating bowls, beakers, and miniature toilet jars. The upper classes who lived in the houses would have used Chinese porcelain bowls and dishes and stoneware jars, or similar vessels in glazed earthenware. Other finds were few: glass and shell beads, small iron knives, bronze eye pencils, and glass bowls and bottles. The people who lived at Gedi were neither wealthy, luxurious nor artistic, but had most of what contributed in their day to good living. "Colonial and comfortable" would be an apt expression for their way of life. Outside the Palace were two large houses: the House of the Chinese Cash and the House of the Porcelain Bowl. The House of the Chinese Cash had been destroyed in the early sixteenth century. In the court a Chinese cash of the Emperor Ning Tsung (A.D. 1195–1224) was found. Copper cash were exported from China, but they have only occurred sporadically in Kenya, always in context much later than the date of the coin. The House of the Porcelain Bowl was small, with only two rooms and a lavatory, built in the ruins of a larger house which had been destroyed by fire. In the back room of the house was found almost complete, a large blue-and-white porcelain bowl in the style of the latter half of the sixteenth century. In the surrounding debris was found in two pieces, the lid of a large jar in dark olive celadon glaze (Plate 3b).

Beyond is the House of the Cistern, a large building with a square court in front and a cistern room used as a bathroom. On the wall of the outer room are a number of graffiti, including a magic square of sixteen numbers used for fortune telling, and some sketches of dhows. The cistern room is a common feature of old-fashioned Arab houses but this is the only example found at Gedi. It seems to have been an amenity that was not introduced until the end of the sixteenth century. There is no drain and the step inside the cistern was used when cleaning it out. It was filled from outside by a channel in the wall so as to avoid any embarrassment which might be caused by failing to knock on the door. The inhabitants of Gedi thought of everything. Behind the House of the

Cistern is the main street running across the town out through the North Gate beyond the Mosque of the Long Conduit. Towards the end of the life of Gedi the street was interrupted by cross walls of obscure purpose.

Leading off the street going north is the House of the Panelled Walls which was rebuilt at a higher level, like the House of the Cistern. It has two large courts in front, an outer room with a lavatory at the end between the two middle rooms and a second lavatory. Strangely enough, there is no sign of a kitchen, unless it be the two rooms cut off from the house with access only to the outer court. Beyond is a rectangular enclosure with a platform at the end and a lavatory, which may have been a Market.

On the opposite side of the street is the Mosque of the Long Conduit. Set in the base of the cistern was found a Chinese blue-and-white porcelain bowl and an Islamic glazed earthenware dish with floral patterns (Plate 3a) both of the early sixteenth century. A large tree had grown in the cistern, effectually hiding and protecting them. On one side of the frame of the qibla were scratched several times the Arabic words *kullu taam* meaning "all food". These are the opening words of the Third Book of the Koran verse 92, which deals with food that is lawful for Muslims. The text reads "All food is lawful unto you which was lawful unto the Israelites and the camel as well". They must be the idle scribblings of a schoolboy when the mosque was being used as a school. It is clear which part of the Koran he considered most memorable.

At the mosque another street turns off to the left at right-angles, parallel to the street behind the Great Mosque. Both streets were laid out in the earliest days of the town and it would appear that Gedi was a deliberate creation, not a haphazard aggregation of houses. Along this street are the House of the Cowries, the House of the Scissors and the House of the Ivory Box. In all of these, pots and some other objects were found on the floors, indicating that some persons had delayed their departure too long. It is curious that they were not collected by the conquerors or by casual visitors before the vegetation began to bring the walls down and the humus to accumulate on the floors.

All ruined sites anywhere in the world, whether an old mine working in America or a crumbling castle on the Danube, are regarded as bad by the local inhabitants, but the spirits of Gedi are considered particularly malign. There is, however, no story of what happened to explain this particular aversion. Something may have occurred beyond the usual atrocities when a town is stormed to create this tradition of horror. Something which our ancestors would have called supernatural and we call natural.

The well shared by the House of the Scissors and the House of the Ivory Box is interesting. Originally it was the old dangerous type of well with the top on which stood the drawer of water at ground level. Later it was converted into a "safety" model with a parapet. This was the beginning of the end.

Beyond these houses is a block consisting of the House of the Iron Lamp, the House of the Sunken Court and the House of the Venetian Bead. The House of the Sunken Court is one of the most elaborate at Gedi. A passage at the end of the street between the House of the Cistern and the House of the Panelled Walls opens into a lobby, with seats round the sides, from which access to the reception court is gained. An inter-communicating room provides access to the reception court from the kitchen, without the necessity of going through the house. In the outer room is an arched recess for drinking water, with a shelf for cups below it. These occur in the Palace and in many of the houses. A more primitive type is a masonry block with a cavity for the base of a jar. The lavatory in this house is double the normal size and it is reached through an anteroom. The house would seem to have had some special function, but nothing was found in it to give any idea of what this could have been.

The House of the Long Conduit is seen behind the Tomb of the Fluted Pillar. In one of the bedrooms of this house was found a fine celadon dish with one piece of the rim missing. The missing part was later found in the store. It must have been at the bottom of a stack of dishes which was taken

12(a) Great Mosque, Gedi: Well,
Conduit and Cistern. Fifteenth
century.

(b) Qibla of Great Mosque,
Gedi. Fifteenth century.

13(a) The Palace, Gedi. Fifteenth century.
(b) Façade of Palace with arches with inverted Y at apex.

from the store. When they were examined it was found to be broken and so it was left behind when the house was cleared. The plate is late fourteenth or early fifteenth century, but sherds of late fifteenth-century porcelain were found on the floor with it.

Outside the area of concentration of buildings are a number of houses and mosques. The most important of those which have been investigated is the block known as the House of the Double Court and the House of the Dhow. In the plaster of the outer room of the House of the Dhow is an incised picture showing the launching of a dhow. This is the only serious attempt at art at Gedi; the other pictures on the walls are just doodlings.

The line of the Inner Wall has been cleared and the path runs along the inner face. It can be seen that it is in fact a barricade in which existing bits of houses have been incorporated. At many points, particularly at the gates and corners, are circular spy holes, and at one place a bastion with a square gunport with splayed sides has been built out to cover an angle of the wall.

Gedi is one of the largest of the surviving Arab colonial towns and the only one maintained as a place of public resort. The reason for the existence of such a large community is still a mystery. It is four miles from the sea and two miles from Mida Creek, a navigable estuary with a difficult entrance, which may have been its port. Near the shore of the creek at a place known as Mgangani are some mounds of rubbish, a well and the remains of a mosque with a finely decorated qibla (Plate 14), resembling the qibla at Rasini in Somalia.

In the days of its prosperity, the fourteenth to sixteenth centuries, there would have been large herds of elephant, rhinoceros, ostrich and giraffe in the neighbourhood, but these would hardly explain the building of such a large town.

It has been suggested that the sea may have retreated, but there is no evidence to support any change in topography. The only change in natural conditions has been a grave fall in the water table which has caused the drying up of the wells.

This may be due to the decline in rainfall, which is suggested by the fall in the Nile levels of the sixteenth century. The low water Niles are dependent on equatorial rains and this decline after a period of exceptionally good rains, covering the fourteenth and fifteenth centuries, with all its consequences, may be an important factor in the decay of civilization in East Africa in the late sixteenth and seventeenth centuries.

The name Gedi, or more correctly Gede, is a Galla personal name meaning "precious". It was the name by which the place was known when the African tribe of the Giriama reoccupied the area when the Galla retreated in the second half of the nineteenth century. It is unlikely to have been its name in the days of its prosperity. It is mentioned in the traditions of the Pokomo, the coastal Bantu tribe who lived in the Tana basin, as Gede Kilimani meaning Gedi on the Hill, a place where a section of the tribe halted for a time in their flight from the Galla. On the Berthelot Map of 1636 in the British Museum a town called Quelmam is shown between Quelife and Malindi, which would appear to be Gedi. This Quelmam could be a Portuguese corruption of Kilimani, one of the commonest place names in East Africa.

Gedi is not mentioned by the Portuguese, nor any town in its vicinity, which is strange considering that the Portuguese were happily settled at Malindi from 1512 to 1593. It is possible that Gedi was destroyed in 1529 by the punitive expedition that is believed to have been sent against Malindi after the sack of Mombasa by Nuno da Cunha, and only reoccupied at the end of the century when the Portuguese were moving to Mombasa.

The quantity of fifteenth-century porcelain found in surface levels suggests that only part of the area was being occupied at the end of the sixteenth century. The absence or scarcity of early sixteenth-century porcelain is not very significant as identifiable early sixteenth-century porcelain is nowhere common. Other hints are offered by the fact that pieces of the same fifteenth-century vessel are found scattered over a large area, which is never the case with the late

sixteenth-century vessels. Another curious fact is the deliberate, but apparently purposeless, alteration of the front
entrance of some of the houses, which suggests that the new
tenants were by no means happy about the attitude of the
spirits of the former owners. If the front door is altered, the
house is no longer the same house, and the homing spirit
does not recognize where he is and goes away.

This conjecture of a destruction of Gedi in the early sixteenth century has still to be confirmed, but it would appear
to have been the only dramatic event in its life. It was founded
probably in the thirteenth century, the earliest sherds are a
glazed earthenware with patterns scratched through the
glaze, known as *sgraffiato*, found under the House of the Dhow.
The only dated monument is a tomb with an inscription
of the Hejira year 802, the equivalent of A.D. 1399, which is
to be seen immediately behind the ticket office. One house,
the House of the Cowries, may date back to the late fourteenth
but Gedi was not much of a place until the middle of the
fifteenth century, when the Great Mosque and Town Wall
were constructed and the town was most prosperous. In the
early sixteenth century, as we have said, it may have been
destroyed by the Mombasans. At the end of the century
there was once more considerable building activity, including
the restoration of the Palace and the Great Mosque and the
construction of the Inner Wall enclosing a much smaller area.
This Indian summer was of short duration, and in the second
quarter of the seventeenth century Gedi was abandoned forever. There is no evidence of anything violent, but that the
evacuation was sudden is shown by the pile of lime in the court
of the Palace Annexe which was being used for plastering
the blocked door. The builders heard that the Galla were
on their way, packed up their belongings and left. Apart
from the trade goods, such as ivory and cloth, these would
not amount to much. Medieval man, even well-to-do man,
had not the personal belongings of a junior clerk of today.

The Galla were a nomadic cattle people and disliked
towns. Their policy was neither exploitation nor assimilation
—it was extermination. The conquered peoples were either

killed and mutilated, or sold as slaves if they were saleable. The Galla had nothing to lose except their lives, their cattle and their women. The Arabs and Bantu retreated before the Galla spearman. Only in the wooded hills behind the coast did the Nyika hold out to prove with their poisoned arrows the superiority of the missile over the shock weapon.

Gedi was abandoned to bush and became a small forest into which only the honey gatherers penetrated. It acquired a particularly bad reputation for ghosts and spirits, possibly due to European encouragement. The coastal African usually endeavours to be co-operative if only he understands what is required of him. Archaeologists are not spiritualists. Since their feet are so firmly on the ground they would have to be giants for their heads to be in the clouds. Nevertheless, when I first started to work at Gedi I had the feeling that something or somebody was looking out from behind the walls, neither hostile nor friendly, but waiting for what he knew was going to happen. Some of the houses have a thick as opposed to a thin, empty or meaningless atmosphere. The something or somebody behind the walls has gone, but some houses still retain for me their peculiar aura.

The coastal African does not only conceive of ghosts as we see them, but he also believes in spirits as creatures in their own right. One of the most unpleasant is a monstrous sheep that follows you wherever you go. One can sympathize with the unpleasantness of having always as a companion the symbol of the essential oneness of the human race.

The ghost stories of the Europeans are mainly associated with inexplicable misfortunes and inconveniences associated with a visit to Gedi. One of the best is of a camping party whose hurricane lamps would not burn and whose torches would not go on, finally the car lamps failed, so they felt they were up against more than they could take and went back to the main road. When they reached the road the lights came on again. This haunting is now a thing of the past. People have camped at Gedi with permission of the authorities and nothing particularly unpleasant or interesting seems to have happened to them which could not have occurred any-

116

where else. The hand of man, even an archaeologist, has restored Gedi to normality. The local inhabitants say that it is still bad, but not as bad as it used to be in the past. This grudging admission concedes more than it reserves. The ghosts of Gedi have gone, yet if you walk round the walls between half past five and six in the evening you may well have all the authentic feelings that precede or accompany an apparition. The things that were not in Horatio's philosophy are still there, though we are living in the best of all materialist eras.

7

Mombasa

THE ISLAND of Mombasa, roughly oval in shape, is a coral atoll rising in places as much as fifty feet above sea level set in one of the indentations of the coast of East Africa. On the north and south the mainland is rather lower than the island, but on the west the ground rises steeply and the island is overlooked by the heights of Chamgamwe and Port Reitz. There are deep water and sheltered anchorages on the north and south sides of the island but on the west, particularly the northwest, the water shallows until it becomes a ford. Here has been built the causeway by which Mombasa is permanently linked to the mainland. The northern harbour is the more sheltered and the more easily accessible to sailing ships, and the old town of Mombasa was built beyond the anchorage. The southern harbour, originally called Tuaca, later Kilindini, was used particularly in the north-east monsoon but never became an independent town.

Mombasa has reasonable water, not as good as Lamu and Malindi but better than most of the other havens. The soil of the island and the immediate mainland is thin and poor though not below the average standard of the coast, and the rainfall is, if anything, less capricious. It was dependent on the mainland or on Pemba and Zanzibar for food.

The word Mombasa is said to be derived from the Arab root *nabas* meaning to speak in public and by implication, a place of congress for purposes other than or as well as trade— a not unreasonable name for a settlement. However, there is no evidence of Mombasa ever having had a status distinct from the other towns of the coast, and there may be another derivation.

It has been said, with more conviction than consideration, that Mombasa is the land of Punt of the Egyptians and the Rhaptum of Ptolemy; nothing has yet appeared apart from words to support such a statement. Archaeological work has hitherto been limited to Fort Jesus and the ruined mosque of the Kilindini, but there has been no lack of utilitarian excavations in the old town of Mombasa and nothing out of mediaeval context has ever appeared. Mombasa is singularly deficient in early traditions and we know virtually nothing about the pre-Portuguese period. It was important at the end of the twelfth century, if the corrupt text of Idrisi can be substantiated. The King of the Zenj is supposed to have lived at Mombasa, though who the King was is unknown, and the description of the bay of Mombasa is so fantastic as to discredit the whole account. The great and prolific Moroccan traveller known as Ibn Batuta spent a night at Mombasa in 1332. He was not received by the Sheikh or ruler and he describes the inhabitants as pious, honourable and upright, which was his way of writing off a people as being without financial or other interest. The greatest of all medieval travellers was one of the worst scroungers, and no contemporary hitch-hiker could have got so much by giving so little as this gentleman from Fez. Admittedly, he was more presentable and his standards were much higher, nevertheless even he was occasionally reduced to pious austerity.

About fifty years before the arrival of the Portuguese the Sheikh of Mombasa was said by the Sheikh of Malindi to have taken the title of Sultan, which alarmed all his colleagues. Previously the only Sultans had been the rulers of Kilwa and Zanzibar, who had an obscure claim by descent from an unidentified Sultan of Shiraz. The size of Mombasa as compared with the other towns is attested by the Portuguese and her aggressive attitude is shown by the pleasure which the other towns, notably Zanzibar and Malindi, took in her misfortunes.

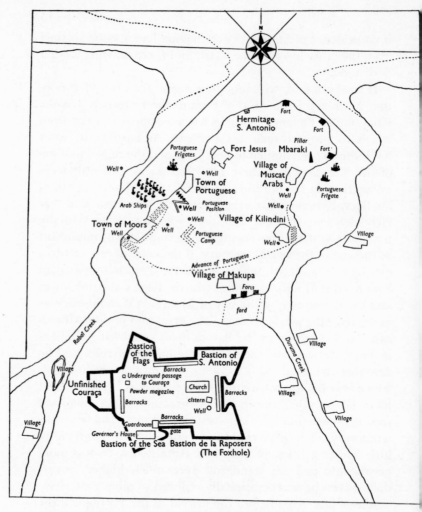

FIG. 9. *Mombasa in* 1728, *with a detailed plan of Fort Jesus at the same date*

Her misfortunes, deserved or not, were grave and repeated, so that nothing has survived of the mediaeval town. The site around the bay, where today mangrove poles are stacked and sharks dried, is well established by the plan of Barreto de Rezende of 1636 and, rather more precisely, by the plan of Engineer-Colonel Lopez de Sá of 1728 (Fig. 9). The town is described as surrounded by a wall and the houses as many-storied, built very close together, with narrow streets between them. Among them were huts with palm frond roofs, where lived the slaves.

At the entrance of the harbour, probably near Mombasa Club, was a fort of which no traces have survived. It was from here that cannon captured from wrecks and served by renegade gunners fired on the Portuguese galleons whenever they attempted to enter the harbour. The fire was invariably ineffective and Mombasa was four times stormed, sacked and burnt. If it had not been permanently occupied at the end of the sixteenth century, this would no doubt have happened again. One admires the unconquerable spirit of the Mombasans but one is disappointed in the resistance they put up when it came to push of pike. The first battle with Francisco d' Almeida on August 15/16, 1505 cost the Portuguese twenty-five to thirty men; the second by Nuno da Cunha on November 17/18, 1528, only one man. On the third and fourth occasion in the early part of 1587 and 1589, the town was forthwith evacuated. On the last occasion in March 1589 the Mombasans had to face a new enemy, a horde of cannibals from the Zambezi known as the Zimba, who had moved north and eaten the inhabitants of Kilwa in 1586. Continuing their culinary progress, they arrived on the mainland opposite Mombasa at the beginning of 1589. At this moment the Mombasans were preparing to welcome the Turkish soldier Mirale Bey on his second visit to East Africa to deliver them from the Portuguese. His more immediate task was obviously to protect them from the cannibals. He sent two of his five ships to hold the Makupa Ford with their cannon, and with the remaining three awaited the Portuguese at the harbour mouth. News of his expedition had reached Goa and a strong fleet under the brother of the Viceroy, Thomé de Sousa Coutinho, was sent to reinforce the Captain of Malindi, Mateus Mendez de Vasconcelos. The Portuguese first captured the three ships in the harbour, then sailed round and sank the two ships at the ford. Another party landed, destroyed the fort at the entrance and occupied the town. The Sheikh of Mombasa, true to form, threatened war, pleaded peace and then fled into the interior of the island. The Portuguese burnt the town after having taken anything of value they could find. This had been the order of events in 1505, 1528–29 and 1587, but this time it was to be followed by a new horror. The cannibals, who had watched with satisfaction the destruction of the defences of the ford, on March 15, swarmed across on to the island and hunted the unfortunate Mombasans out of the thickets and palm groves where they had taken refuge from the Portuguese. Back to the burning town fled the Mombasans, and then into the sea, where some were rescued by the Portuguese. Never could there have been such a demonstration of being between the devil and the deep blue sea. Among them fled Mirale Bey and his captains, who were picked up by the Portuguese with some of the leading citizens of Mombasa.

Mirale Bey showed more skill in the handling of his misfortunes than he had done in war. It was clear that diplomacy, rather than fighting, was his rightful profession. Early in his life, he had been captured by the Spaniards and had learnt to make himself understood and acceptable. When he was brought before the King of Malindi and told to behave with respect, he remarked that he would be truly an ass if he behaved like a horse in his asinine position. He did better at Goa when brought before the Viceroy. When asked how he felt, he replied, "A slave of your Highness and as such the greater Lord." Finally, when transferred to Lisbon he became a Christian and, as a rather naive chronicler remarks, gained for his soul what he had lost of earthly things. Actually he seems to have done very well by both this world and the next, or at least to have made the most of life's discourtesies. His friends and foes were not so fortunate or adaptable. His captive Roque de Brito, Captain of Malindi, had not the same versatility and died a prisoner in Istambul. The Sheikh of Lamu who had handed over Roque de Brito, the brother of the Sheikh of Kilifi who had joined him, and the two emissaries from Pate who had come to fetch him, were publicly beheaded and quartered at Pate.

Africa was always a land of opportunity and there have been few brighter opportunists than Mirale Bey. There were, however, very few Muslims who emulated him. One wonders if he was not the son of a Christian mother, forced into a harem and then neglected, so that her son had little sense of loyalty to the institutions in which he had been brought up. There were Arabs and Swahili who remained loyal to the Portuguese in their darkest hours but they also remained pious Muslims. Christian renegades were not uncommon, usually from the lower ranks. Some apostasized to save their skins and returned to their faith as soon as they could. A few seem to have done so to forward their fortunes, such as the scoundrelly ex-Captain of Mombasa Simão de Mello Pereira, but seldom with the grace of Mirale Bey.

The cannibals left Mombasa and marched north to destruction at Malindi. The derelict town then seems to have been occupied by the Sheikh of Kilifi who installed his brother as Sheikh of Mombasa. He did not, however, last long. The Sheikh of Kilifi had attacked the Sheikh of Malindi but was defeated and killed by his allies, the African tribe of the Segeju. The Segeju continued their victorious campaign, defeated and killed the new Sheikh of Mombasa and occupied the town. They were not interested in towns and handed over the new acquisition to the Sheikh of Malindi.

The Portuguese decided to invest their old ally, the Sheikh of Malindi with Mombasa and to build a fortress for themselves so as to extinguish forever an inveterate centre of disaffection. It is strange that the Portuguese had been so slow to make a base of the finest harbour on the coast of East Africa. One reason was the well justified reluctance on the part of the Viceroy, in view of his limited resources of manpower and munitions, to take on a new commitment which in view of the existence of Malindi seemed hardly necessary. The other may have been the unhealthiness of Mombasa island. Nuno da Cunha had spent the winter of 1528–29 at Mombasa and had lost between 300 to 400 men. As Dr. Axelson has remarked, Africa has a way of repaying death with death. Today things are very different and one's chances of dying of a local disease in Mombasa are little less than perishing from a ghostly Portuguese musket ball.

However, the two raids of Mirale Bey, and the appearance of the Netherlanders in the Indian Ocean, swung the balance in favour of strong points as opposed to diplomatic arrangements. The fact that Fort Jesus eventually fell is no argument that the new policy was ill-founded. The Dutch fleets that were tearing the Portuguese Empire to pieces would have made short work of the unfortified factory at Malindi. They never attacked Fort Jesus.

The establishment of the Portuguese and the Sheikh of Malindi in Mombasa necessitated the rebuilding of the town, and the development of the area between the Fort and the old town wall and the harbour. This became the residential quarter of the Portuguese and some of the streets, such as Ndia Kuu, are on the old courses. The principal buildings were the Convent of the Augustinians, the Parish church and the Church of the Misericordia. These have all disappeared. They are mentioned by Guillain in 1846 but he does not describe exactly where they were situated. The traditional site is the house of Hassanali Mohamedali Noorbhai and the Hanafiya Mosque built about 1854 at the north end of Ndia Kuu.

The Palace of the new Sultan was outside the Arab town. It is possible that this is the isolated house with a well to the north-west of the Fort shown on the Rezende plan. The two houses on the Lopez de Sá plan, described as "houses of Miguel de Faria" are in the same position. It was not far from the Fort because on one occasion the Portuguese Captain fired on it. The watch-tower, which is eccentrically placed in the north curtain wall of the Fort, must have been sited to keep a particular spot in the town under observation, and what spot could there be other than the Palace.

The whole interest of Mombasa during the later Portuguese period and during most of the succeeding Mazrui period is centred in Fort Jesus. It was within the walls of the Fort that the decisions were taken and afterwards fought out, that made the history of what is now Kenya, Tanganyika and Zanzibar. The busy commercial town had disappeared with the cannibal feast and until the slow revival of prosperity in the second half of the nineteenth century, the town of Mombasa was an appendage of the fortress. The commerce that did go on was engrossed first by the Portuguese Captain and then by his Omani, and later Zanzibari successor. The words of William Alley written in 1661, "If there was any business worth anything it would be seized by the Governor", were echoed by Von Decken speaking of the "poor Tanggai" two hundred years later.

South and south-west of Fort Jesus there is a series of forts along the edge of the cliff between the two harbours of Mombasa proper, named by the Portuguese Rio de Santo Antonio and Kilindini. There were also two other structures, the Hermitage of Nossa Senhora da Esperança and beside it a cross fifteen feet high, which served as a leading mark for vessels coming in from the sea whether they were entering the northern or southern harbour. The Hermitage and Cross are shown on the Rezende Map of 1636, the forts on the maps of 1728. The most important of these is a large semicircular redoubt with embrasures for cannon at the end of Ras Serani, covering the place where the two channels meet. It is impossible to see it as anything but the redoubt that was restored in anticipation of the Omani attack of 1826. Today this is known as Fort St. Joseph, but on the plan of Lopez de Sá it is shown as the fortified Hermitage. On the slope behind the redoubt was at one time a building with a stone lintel over the gate which, from a photograph, would appear to have been Portuguese and was probably the Hermitage from which the redoubt got its name. An inscribed stone, illegible except for the date 1677, is in the Law Courts at Mombasa and came from this site. During the siege it was the cannon in this redoubt, manned by a renegade Portuguese named Nunes, that was the most effective.

The battery behind was constructed at the beginning of the 1939–45 war, and steps leading down to a passage were discovered during building operations. However, it was no time for research and the passage was not followed. There

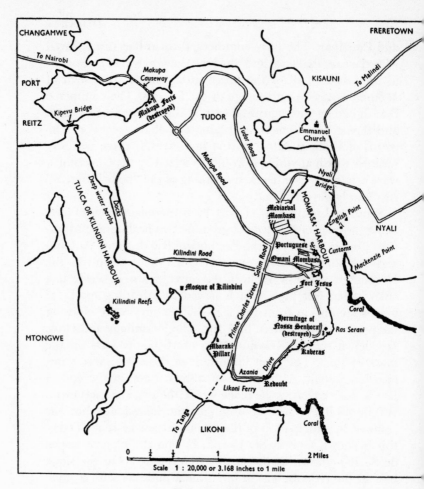

FIG. 10. *Mombasa*

is a story, believed by many, that a secret passage ran from Fort St. Joseph to Fort Jesus. It is not mentioned by the Portuguese, which I suppose is logical enough if it was a secret. On the other hand, it would have been a major operation to construct it and an unnecessarily cumbrous way of providing communications with the outside world for a beleaguered garrison. During a siege supplies and reinforcements could always be landed on the shore below

126

the Fort and brought into it through a passage in the rock below the gun platform.

Near the redoubt a flight of steps leads down to a cave which is partially filled at high water. At the back and above the roof of the cave is a small chamber with a square air vent in the roof which could have served as a hideout. The cave was examined by Thornton and Von Decken in 1861, who said that it would be invisible from the sea. Surrounded by a fence and with a brushwood hut on top of it, it would be equally invisible from the land. In fact it would serve admirably for the smuggling business which can flourish at any time and any place. There is no evidence to date it, but it is interesting that the installation was abandoned or at least only occasionally used in Von Decken's day. It would seem most likely to belong to the early period of the rule of Seyyid Said, when the Mazrui had been disposed of and Mombasa was under what was still a new and alien regime. Eventually somebody gave the smugglers away and the huts were removed.

The Cross is shown on the plans of Rezende (1636) and Lopez de Sá (1728) and is mentioned by Von Decken in 1861. It was seen by New in 1868 but he mentions that it disappeared soon after.

Further along the cliff in the middle of the golf course are the remains of an oval-shaped structure which is called today the Chapel of Nossa Senhora but is marked on the Portuguese plan as the Fort of S. José. Guillain marks it as the "Kaberas", named in honour of an Arab warship of Seif bin Sultan whose crew stormed the redoubt. When the Muscat fleet entered Kilindini Harbour in 1696, the flagship struck a sand bank and swung round so that the two bow guns pointed directly at it. After a few rounds the Swahili garrison fled, followed by the Portuguese gunners after they had spiked the guns. It must have been disconcerting to find your enemies guns laid "dead on" by Providence. It is probably this incident which is commemorated.

At the end of the golf course is another redoubt covering the entrance of Kilindini Harbour. This is a position shown on the Portuguese maps. Finally there were the remains of a redoubt near the Mbaraki Pillar covering the creek where the Yacht Club has its headquarters.

The construction of all these forts in the second half of the seventeenth century shows the concern felt in Goa for the position in East Africa, though it is strange, considering the chronic shortage of man-power, that they should have thought that they would be able to man them. They could not prevent a disembarkation on the island, and the scattered units would be in grave danger of being cut off from the main garrison in Fort Jesus.

Another fortified area was the ford at Makupa across which the cannibals had swarmed. The cannibals had gone but the African tribe of the Mosungalos, probably a vanished branch of the north-east Bantu, was a continual nuisance. Three blockhouses were built by the Portuguese on the low ground below the cliff to watch the ford. They were garrisoned by a small unit under a sergeant but the protection does not seem to have been very effective, and it is possible that this unit had a commercial and political as well as military function. In 1612 and 1614, there were incursions on to the island and in 1625 the Governor, Francisco de Sousa Pereira, was killed by raiders from the mainland. The Mosungalos gave valuable help to Dom Jeronimo in 1632. They continued their invasions and in 1667 sacked the town. During the siege they were usually on the side of the Portuguese. On one occasion, they ambushed a party leaving the Hermitage and presented thirty Arab heads to the Captain of the Fort as a proof of loyalty. An Arab punitive expedition sent against them ended in disaster, but their attacks on the Arab redoubt were not effective. They were in fact more dangerous to their enemies than helpful to their friends. The blockhouses have now all disappeared but a curious bas-relief, with an illegible inscription surmounted by a crown which was on one of the walls, was drawn by Von Decken.

The only other notable building probably of the Portuguese period which has survived is a hollow conical shaped tower with light vents in the sides, standing about twenty-five feet

14. Qibla of Mosque, Mgangani, near Gedi. Uncertain date.

15. Pillar at Mbáraki, Mombasa. Late seventeenth century.

high above the creek at Mbaraki (Plate 15). It is shown on the plans of 1728 but not on the Rezende plan of 1636. It is probably the tomb of the first sheikh of Wa-Kitoue, a component of the Chamgamwe tribe, one of the Three Tribes, who came on to the island after the depopulation in the sixteenth century, mentioned by Guillain.

8

Fort Jesus

F ORT JESUS, Mombasa, rises from a coral ridge that runs
down to the mouth of the harbour at the point where ships
entering or leaving at low water must keep close to the
southern shore to avoid the currents of the central channel
or the shoals of the north mainland (see Frontispiece). The
site of the Fort is cut off from the ridge behind it by a ditch
ten feet deep and varying from thirty to ten feet wide. The
rock below the walls has been cut back to a near vertical
face, so that two-thirds of the ramparts are solid coral. This
meant that the walls could not be breached or undermined.
Before the days of high explosive the Fort, if adequately
garrisoned, could only have been taken by escalade and this
obviously meant heavy casualties. No one, except perhaps
the incredible soldiers of Wellington's army in the Peninsular
War, is very enthusiastic about operations in which most
of the honours will be posthumous.

The architect was an Italian João Batista Cairato who,
after working on the fortifications of Milan and Malta, was
sent to India. For thirteen years he worked in the Portuguese possessions in the East as Chief Architect of India.
His last assignment was Fort Jesus and the plan of the Fort
today, apart from the gatehouse and the elliptical bastion
covering the gate, is his work. The most striking features are
the two landward bastions, S. Phelipe and S. Alberto, with
their deep re-entrant angles by which the curtain wall

130

between them and the opposite faces of the bastions could be swept with enfilade fire. The gate on the north side of the Fort was covered by two gunports in the opposite flank of S. Phelipe. The seaward face was designed with a rectangular projecting gun-platform and swept back flanks (the seaward bastions of S. Matias and S. Mateus) to give as wide a field of fire as possible. There are two small blind spots, the north-west corner of S. Phelipe and the south-west corner of S. Alberto, which are not covered by the salients of S. Matias and S. Mateus. Otherwise it is a model fortress in which each part contributes to the defence of its neighbour.

It changed hands nine times: twice by trickery in 1631 and 1828; twice by escalade in 1698 and 1746 when the defenders were insufficient to man the walls; twice by starvation in 1729 and 1828; once by bombardment with rockets and shell in 1875, and twice by negotiation in 1728 and 1837.

The original ramparts consisted of a wall, fourteen feet thick, surmounted by a parapet four feet six inches high and eight feet thick. Behind the parapet was a parapet walk and firing step, rising an average three feet above the level of the ground inside the Fort (Plate 17b). On the seaward side, the original parapet is obscured by later work, but it would appear to have been different.† The gate was in the position of the present gate, though the inscription must have been placed above it after the date of the dedication April 11, 1593. Mateus Mendes de Vasconcelos only left Malindi on January 10, and it is unlikely, even in the present days of crash and brash development, that the walls of the Fort could have reached this height in such a short time. Inside the Fort were a Chapel, cistern, barrack rooms and a Captain's house. Excavations in the Fort have uncovered a fourteen-foot-wide

† Excavations have revealed an eleven-foot wide flight of steps against the south wall of the gun-platform, leading down to a five-foot gate in the outer wall of the Fort. They had been filled in not later than the middle of the seventeenth century, and may have been merely constructional. The original south wall of the gun-platform was a plain curtain without firing step or offensive facilities.

131

passage cut in the coral and spanned by round arches, descending towards the couraça or outwork outside the Fort where the heavy guns would be sited.

Outside the walls, the foundations of the padrão or pillar shown on the Texeira plan (Fig. 11a) have also been revealed with the cannon balls of Francesco de Moura's bombardment sticking in it.

The Fort was surrounded by a dry ditch which was never finished and the overhanging counterscarp was allowed to remain, although to break it back would have involved comparatively little work. This was a blessing for the two thousand civilians who are said to have taken refuge in the ditch during the first years of the siege.

On the outside of the four corner bastions were the arms of the persons whose names had decided which of the saints were to be associated with Fort Jesus. On the north-west corner is the shield of Philip I of Portugal at whose orders the Fort was built. Philip I of Portugal was the Philip II of Spain who had inherited the Kingdom of Portugal on the death of King Sebastian at the disastrous battle of Alcacer al Kebir in 1580. In the south-west are the arms of the Archduke of Austria known as Albert the Pious, Archbishop of Toledo and Regent of Portugal from 1594-96. On the south-east are the arms of Mateus Mendes de Vasconcelos, the builder of the Fort, probably the ablest Portuguese officer to serve in East Africa (Plate 16b). Only the north-east bastion has lost its arms, which were those of Matias d'Albuquerque Viceroy of India 1590–97 in whose period of office the Fort was built. This escutcheon is not mentioned by Guillain and may have been destroyed in one of the many bombardments of Seyyid Said in the early nineteenth century. The Fort was in a sense built by the end of the tour of duty of Vasconcelos in 1596, but the ditch was still shallow, the walls were low and there was no proper gate, only apparently a wicket gate in the wall, reached across a wooden bridge.

The amicable relations which Vasconcelos had maintained with everyone, except on one occasion with his commanding officer over the awkward question of prize money, did not survive his departure. There was a chronic shortage of money in a country that was no Mexico or Peru, and the pernicious system by which the Portuguese officials bought their office and then tried to recoup themselves out of the perquisites and privileges tended to apply the acid test of *meo bono* to every issue that arose. In a short time there were arguments over the share of the 6 per cent customs duty that was to go to the Sultan, the trading privileges he should enjoy as Sultan and brother in arms of the King of Portugal, and the obscure claim to the island of Pemba.

In 1606 the Sultan conquered Pemba with his own troops and his position was recognized on condition that a tribute in rice was paid. Three years later, the old King Ahmad died and was succeeded by his son Hasan, but the rights and honours which the old King had been granted or, one might say, won by persistent moaning and arguing, were not automatically to pass to his heirs. They would have presumably to show the same forensic stamina that their father had done. This was an order from Lisbon, and the Viceroy, as a professional local administrator, saw all the troubles inherent in it. It was not until 1612 that the Sultan received from Lisbon a letter informing him that he had been granted one-third share of the customs but this was a special favour to him and would not necessarily be granted to his heirs.

However, the situation in Mombasa was worsening on its own and no outside fuel was necessary. The Captain of the time, Manuel de Mello Pereira, exceeded his predecessors in arrogance and extortion, and the Sultan broke off relations with him and ceased to visit the Fort. The affair was exasperated by a villainous uncle of the Sultan called by the Portuguese Munganja, who took advantage of the situation to further his own designs on the Sultanate. The "loyal" Munganja clamoured at the gates of the Fort, saying that his life was in danger because of his love of the Portuguese. The Captain, perhaps feeling for once that he might have right on his side, opened fire on the Palace. The Sultan retired to Kilifi and waited for the air to cool, hoping that Munganja might overplay his hand.

While the Sultan and Captain had been fighting, the African tribe on the mainland beyond the ford, the Mosungalos, had become restive. They were accustomed to receiving presents of cloth and iron, partly to maintain trade contacts and partly to keep them from raiding the island and plundering those who had something to lose. This symbiotic relationship, similar to that which prevailed in the bad old days of cannon diplomacy on the north-west frontier of India and which prevails today in the enlightened atmosphere of mutual help in the oil-bearing countries of the Middle East, had been interrupted, probably by the determination of the Captain to lose nothing of the profit he hoped to get from his captaincy. The Mosungalos crossed the Ford saying that they had come to drive out the usurper Munganja. They tried to avoid fighting with the Portuguese, but in a skirmish some soldiers were killed. The Sultan then returned and a truce was patched up while both sides waited until the ship from Goa should arrive with the Viceroy's reply to their complaints against each other. The Sultan was not without friends among the Portuguese and the civil official next to the Captain, Antonio de Cunha, endeavoured to keep the peace between them.

Early in 1614 the ship with the fatal decision arrived. The Sultan was exonerated, but he was to be arrested and brought to Goa so as to make an impression on the coast of East Africa. The execution of this face-saving order was entrusted to Simão de Mello Pereira, who was sent to replace Manuel de Mello Pereira as Captain of Mombasa at the end of his tour of duty. The Sultan, however, was on his guard and when summoned to the Fort fled to his African friends the Mosungalos. At Arabaja, the present Rabai, where later Krapf was to build his mission, his hosts were bribed with two thousand pieces of cloth to murder him. His head was sent to Mombasa and forwarded to Goa as a hard-won trophy, which, I suppose from the point of view of a hard-up Captain, it was. The murdered Sultan had behaved with scrupulous rectitude and good sense, but his virtues had helped him no more than many others in similar situations.

This disgraceful deed was thoroughly disapproved in

Lisbon, but professional loyalty in Goa succeeded in covering up their guilty brother. This unmitigated scoundrel in fact enjoyed two tours at Fort Jesus and was only moved to Ormuz in 1620. After the loss of that fortress to the Omanis, he was tried in absence and condemned to death, but he escaped, fled to the Arabs and became a Muslim. The use of the established channels of discipline too often led to the guilty getting off scot free. Less law would have produced more justice.

The Council of State at Lisbon succeeded in blocking the succession of Munganja. Eventually the murdered Hasan's son Yusuf, who had been educated as a Christian in Goa and trained as a gunner, returned to Mombasa twelve years after the death of his father as Dom Jeronimo Chingulia. Early in 1626 he was installed as Sultan of Mombasa, Malindi and Pemba, and the stage was set for the next tragedy. He was then a young man of about twenty with a good record of active service in the Persian Gulf under the distinguished soldier Ruy Frey de Andrade. He was married to a Portuguese Goan and had adopted the Christian religion and way of life. The judge Pedro Alvares Pereira reported well of him, but Pereira was as critical of his countrymen abroad and as tolerant of anybody else as any left-wing politician today. The Arab chronicle of Mombasa mentions with disgust that he ate pork and forced others to eat pork with him.

Nevertheless, whatever he did or did not do, his position was, to say the least, invidious. He was an Arab Sultan, the son of an Arab Sultan, and the leader of the King of Portugal's loyal East African subjects. However, he could not identify himself with them since he had abandoned the true faith and their way of living. On the other hand, the Portuguese either could not or would not regard him as one of themselves or treat him with the respect he considered his due. He was no doubt a tiresome young man and the two Portuguese captains he had to deal with were unfriendly and overbearing. A sidelight on the miserable state of intrigue to Mombasa is indicated by the fact that the Portuguese who reported to the Captain that he had seen the King praying at his father's tomb went to the King and warned him that he had been seen. Dom Jeronimo knew how to deal with persons of this type. He thanked his well-wisher warmly and had him murdered on the way home—shades of Rosencrantz and Guildenstern. But this was not enough. He realized the deadly peril in which he stood. As a relapsed convert he would be sent back to Goa to face the Inquisition, and his chances of getting off would be small. His father had been a man of peace and had retired from the conflict when it was too much for him. He had been murdered, as a result of his forbearance. The Mosungalos would murder anybody for a few bales of cloth and his fellow Arabs, who looked on him with horror, would cut his throat in exchange for a trading permit. He was a soldier and a man of action; he would act differently.

The next morning, April 15, 1631 and the Feast of the Assumption of the Virgin Mary, he came to the Fort with his followers to pay his respects to the Captain. As Pedro Leitão de Gamboa rose to greet him he drew a dagger from his robe and killed him, and his followers fell upon the unprepared Portuguese before they knew what was happening. In the space of a few minutes he was master of the Fort. The Portuguese, principally women and children, who were outside the Fort in their houses, took refuge in the Augustinian Convent. They were offered the usual choice of becoming Muslims or death, and all except one chose death. The wife and the daughter of the Captain were killed either in the Chapel on the day of the revolt or two days later. There are several circumstantial accounts of what occurred, which differ in detail but not in essentials. They all record the steadfastness of the women and the hysterical behaviour of Dom Jeronimo who insulted the corpse of the dead and desecrated the altars of the churches. Sixty Portuguese with an unspecified number of women and children were killed in the massacre, including Dom Jeronimo's brother-in-law and father-in-law. His wife was locked up and treated worse than a slave.

Dom Jeronimo had returned to the faith of his fathers with a vengeance, and in successful action presumably found some satisfaction. The Portuguese in India were in desperate straits but they got together a large expedition which arrived in Mombasa on January 10, 1632. It was neither well trained nor disciplined and the walls of the fortress with guns directed by an experienced gunner were too much for it. After losing many men in forays from their camp at Kilindini they broke off the siege and withdrew at the beginning of March.

Yusuf, now veering again towards Dom Jeronimo, had had enough of Mombasa and, finding life with his fellow Arabs as distasteful as life with the Portuguese, sailed away in a captured galleon with the guns of the Fort and became a pirate. In the course of his wanderings up and down the east coast he captured a Dominican friar and took the opportunity to write an *apologia pro vita*. This time there was no nonsense about conversion or death for the friar, or the true religion of Islam for himself, but a lot about his rights and the indignities he suffered from the captains of Mombasa. He appears never to have got away from his Christian education, and would in fact have been quite happy as a Portuguese Othello fighting the battles of Portugal in the Persian Gulf, hob-nobbing with his fellow gunners and their women in Goa, and making an occasional donation to the Misericordia. The end came six years later. Chased up and down the East African and Hadhramaut coasts, he went up the Red Sea and died at Jedda after a fight with some fellow Arabs.

Little information has come down to reconstruct the society in Mombasa that came to an end on August 15, 1631. There would be at the top the Captain, his wife and daughter and on another eminence the Christian Sultan and his wife. Grouped around were the Augustinian Prior and the other clerics, the Judge, and the Factor or Customs Officer. Outside the official circle, there would be the small group of *entrepreneurs* struggling to maintain themselves inside and outside the Captain's monopolies. Finally at the bottom were the soldiers—Portuguese, Spanish and a few German gungers—with their Eurasian wives and African mistresses. The civilians would have lived in the houses in the town, the clerics in the Augustinian Convent. The pattern of social

137

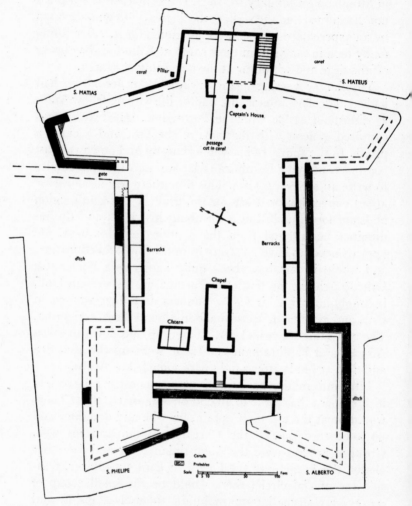

FIG. 11a. *Fort Jesus before reconstruction of* 1634

life would be a faint imitation of Goa; wire pulling, gossip, gambling and amorous intrigues, without the opportunities which existed in the capital city.

138

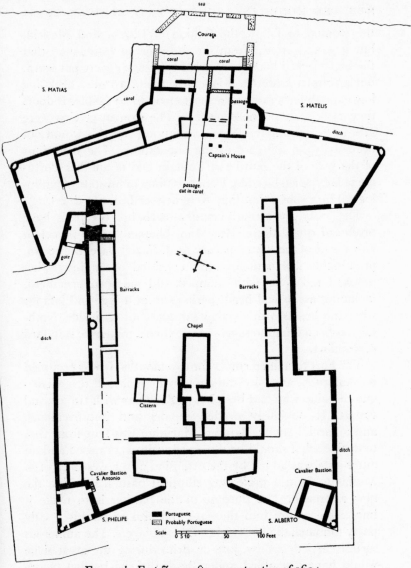

sea

Couraça

coral coral

coral

S. MATIAS

coral

passage

S. MATEUS

ditch

Captain's House

passage
cut in coral

gate

Barracks

Barracks

N

Chapel

ditch

Cistern

ditch

Cavalier Bastion
S. Antonio

Cavalier Bastion

S. PHELIPE

■ Portuguese
▦ Probably Portuguese

S. ALBERTO

Scale 0 5 10   50   100 Feet

FIG. 11*b*. *Fort Jesus after reconstruction of* 1634

The clothes worn by the men out of doors consisted of short
tight-fitting jackets and baggy trousers fastened at the ankles,
and a felt hat with a narrow brim rather like a bowler. Inside
their homes they wore pyjamas. One would have expected

139

the women to follow the fashion of Lisbon and Madrid, but it would appear from the drawings of Linschoten that the high-necked bodice and wide farthingale were not worn, but a simpler costume, a long gown with a round neck-line low enough for a cross on a short chain to be visible. Indoors they wore a diaphanous negligé. The women of Goa were said to be extremely idle and licentious, but this would not necessarily be the case in the out-stations. The behaviour of the wife of the murdered Captain and of another Portuguese lady when faced by Dom Jeronimo in his state of pathological fury shows that they were neither frail nor timid.

The early seventeenth-century levels in Fort Jesus have produced quantities of late Ming blue-and-white porcelain and a little of the contemporary Arab glazed ware. European, presumably Portuguese, wares consisted of an interesting polished red ware with stamped and moulded ornament, including a classical head, perhaps from a jug, and jars for wine and basins with a yellow salt glaze on the inside. Nothing has been found to suggest more than a moderate standard of comfort.

The Fort remained empty for two months. It was occupied on August 5, 1632 by the captain designate Pedro Rodrigues Botelho who had been left at Zanzibar with two coastal vessels. It obviously needed repairs and improvements, and a special envoy, Baltasar Marinho, was sent from Goa to decide what should be done. All walls were raised and an outer gate was added by the extension of the west face of S. Matias to form a projecting elliptical bastion covering the new approach. The purpose of the bastion is to make it impossible to fire into the gate and also to permit a sally party to marshall out of sight of the besiegers. The numerous sorties carried out by José de Brito during the great siege would have assembled under the lee of the bastion before rushing out to assail the Arab earthworks. A second gate was built in front of the first (Plate 16a). The seafront was remodelled by the addition of towers in the angles of the gun-platform and the two seaward bastions. The Captain's house ran over the Passage of the Arches but only the east wall seems to have survived. Two pillars of the portico on the west are built into the later House of the Mazrui. Other works which were recommended included the raising of the outer wall so that the house was no longer visible from the sea.

The inscription of Francisco de Seixas Cabreira on the gate mentions the construction of the gatehouse and the repair of the Fort. Francisco de Seixas Cabreira was the captain who succeeded Botelho, and when he retired in 1639 he recorded on the gatehouse all that he had accomplished and the honours he had received during his tour of duty. He did not undervalue himself, nevertheless it is possible that the restoration of the Portuguese position in East Africa was due to his energy and determination.

Something like the old order returned to Mombasa. A number of outlying Portuguese merchants and beachcombers were ordered to live in the town to re-establish a European community. The Arab and Swahili community was reinforced from Malindi and Kilifi, now rapidly falling into decay as a result of the southern advance of the Galla. It is probable that the Arab-African tribe of the Kilindini, who had originally fled from the Somali before the Galla and who had been living on the mainland, now moved on to the island. Although invited, they had refused to move, so long as there was an Arab Sultan, for fear that they would be reduced to servitude.

The seventeenth century was a period of great distress in Goa. Every misfortune that could occur—plague, famine, blockade and war—assailed the former "Queen of the East". Little help was sent or could be sent to East Africa. The Fort is described in an inscription of 1648 as being greatly dilapidated. In this year it was repaired and a cavalier bastion, S. Antonio, was built inside the old S. Phelipe. A "cavalier" bastion was a bastion that overlooked the others, as a horseman overlooked a footman. It was provided with battlements on the inside and was approached by a flight of steps but had no roof. Another inscription, which has been lost, was recorded by Von Decken and referred to a rebuilding

141

of "a bastion S. Angelo" and the whole parapet of the perimeter, as well as the digging of a well inside the Fort by a
Captain José. This would appear to be Captain José Homem
da Costa 1671–73; the bastion S. Angelo may be a mistake
for S. Antonio, though it must have been very badly built
to need repairing after only twenty-three years. The construction of the wall with the musket slits above the old coping
in the bastion of S. Alberto could be the rebuilding mentioned
in the inscription. The finds in the undisturbed section of the
raised parapet walk, which is associated with this wall,
would not be inconsistent with a date in the third-quarter
of the seventeenth century.

Curiously enough there is no mention in the records of the
reconstruction of the chapel which became the Parish Church
of Mombasa, the *madre sé* or *yglesia paroquial* of the eighteenth-
century plans. The altar was moved to the east end and a
new entrance made at the west, which was approached
through a double court backing on to the south block of
barrack rooms. The north block was destroyed before the
court was built. Drains were made to take rain water from the
roof of the chapel to the adjacent cistern (Plate 17a).

There are no dated plans between 1636 and 1728. The two
eighteenth-century plans do not agree and one of them may
be earlier. The Cienfuegos plan was made by an adventurer
who called himself the Marquis of Cienfuegos, but in official
Portuguese circles he was said to be the son of a servant of the
Duchess de Aveiro and a renegade Carmelite friar. The
Lopez de Sá plan was made by a Portuguese Engineer
Colonel Lopez de Sá, a more respectable person. Both had
taken part in the fortunate expedition of 1728, so they had
actually seen the Fort.

The Lopez de Sá plan (Fig. 9) shows the difference in
level between the floors of the bastions of S. Phelipe, S.
Alberto and S. Mateus and the central court, two "cavalier"
bastions with guardrooms attached, and a building in S.
Matias. It also has a scale which inspires confidence. However, the chapel is shown much shorter than it is in actuality,
and the building at the east end of the court is left out entirely.

Its contemporaneity is proved by the text which refers to the "well made by the Arabs". The omission of the building at the east end of the court is explicable, if this building was in ruins and was only restored by the Arabs when they added the upper story later in the eighteenth century. The chapel is a more difficult problem. When the Portuguese re-entered the Fort they describe the chapel as intact, while excavations have shown no signs of a cross wall or any modifications affecting its length.

The Cienfuegos plan, in spite of its schematic character and its dubious author, may be more accurate. The proportions of the chapel are correctly shown, and so far I have been unable to fault the bogus marquis, except in the absence of cavalier bastions. The plan would appear to have been taken from the archives in Goa and to show the Fort in the middle of the seventeenth century. It should then be compared with the Rezende rather than with the Lopez de Sá plan. The main differences are the disappearance of the central blocks, the addition of a barrack block at the west end of the court, a house *casa del gobernador* in the Matias bastion, the inner gate, and a well to the north of the cistern, which may be the S. André well mentioned in the lost inscription.

In 1650 the great fortress of Muscat in Oman, on which the position of Portugal in the Persian Gulf had depended since the loss of Ormuz, was taken. In the harbour several Portuguese ships had been captured and in a short time the Omanis had a European type of fleet which could meet the Portuguese on even terms. The energetic Francisco de Seixas Cabreira was sent back to Mombasa and for a time restored or rather maintained the *status quo*. But in February 1661 the Omanis sacked the town and captured three Portuguese ships in the harbour, though they did not dare to attack the Fort. Civil war in Oman postponed the final trial of strength and in 1678 and 1687 Pate, which had become the centre of resistence, was punished with old-time severity.

The economic state of Mombasa at this time is difficult to evaluate. It is possible that the loss of the coast to the north, except when there was a punitive expedition in operation,

contributed by the freeing of controls to the general prosperity. The poverty and lack of resources of the central
government at Goa was a byeword throughout the East
but, as Boxer has pointed out, the churches of Goa are evidence
of money for spending, and that someone made money is
shown by the private contributions that were forthcoming
in times of calamity—(a rich widow, Aldonça Gomes, helped
to keep alive the thousands packed in the ditch of Fort Jesus
during the great siege). There is no decline in the quantity
and quality of the porcelain found in the Fort and fragments
of about a hundred bowls and jars of *famille verte* were
found in the deposit of this period in the Bastion of S. Phelipe.
The economic strength of the Portuguese in the East had been
driven into hiding by the rules and monopolies but it had not
been completely destroyed. Even today, with the vastly
improved methods of modern financial control and the
strength and watchfulness of the trade unions, some persons
continue to make considerable sums of money. The spirit of
man is unconquerable.

The gathering storm broke in March 1696, when a fleet of
seven Omani ships, a number of dhows from Pate and Lamu,
and a force of three thousand men arrived to take the Fort.
After a brief artillery dual with the forts at Ras Serani, the
Arab fleet entered Mombasa Harbour and landed their
troops. The Portuguese Captain, João Rodrigues Leão, was
an experienced soldier who had been expecting the attack,
and had made all possible arrangements for a long siege.
He had not more than seventy Portuguese but there were a
large number of pro-Portuguese Swahili, said to be several
thousands. The fighters were allowed into the Fort; the non-
combatants were accommodated outside in the ditch. It
was considered that the Fort was more important than transi-
tory human occupants, and only persons who could con-
tribute to its defence had any right to its protection. In
those undemocratic days there was no sentimental valuation
of human life.

The siege was not at first pressed. The Arabs set up a
number of positions to surround the Fort, which they bom-

barded ineffectually. A member of the garrison, José Barroso, got out and returned three months later with reinforcements numbering twenty-eight Portuguese and forty-six African slaves. Supplies were sent by sea by Fatima, the pro-Portuguese Queen of Zanzibar, and on payment by the African tribes living on the mainland. In August the Omani Commander returned to Oman with the bulk of his forces and a good stock of ivory.

Military superiority had passed temporally to the Portuguese but the Captain, now a sick man, did not consider himself strong enough to take the offensive. On October 23, he died and was succeeded by the next ranking official, a civilian António Mogo de Mello, the head of the recently formed trading company. Mogo de Mello was criticized for being lacking in energy and a poor disciplinarian, in that he allowed soldiers to visit the women in the ditch and catch venereal disease from them. I very much doubt if any commanders of the seventeenth century, except Oliver Cromwell, considered themselves entitled to interfere with the recreations of their troops. However, he had not much opportunity to show initiative as in the middle of December the Arab forces were strongly reinforced and the siege was pressed with a new determination. The garrison was now down to twenty Portuguese and the defence depended on the faithful Swahili. Ingenious attempts to undermine the confidence of the Portuguese in the extraordinary loyalty of their comrades were countered with skill by Mogo de Mello. The leader of the loyalists, Faqih Ali, offered to be blown from a gun if there was any truth in the story put about by the Arabs that he had promised to surrender the fortress to them. Mogo de Mello publicly accepted his denial and decreed death to anybody who should question his fidelity. The devotion of the Swahili loyalists, almost to a man Muslim, to the Portuguese and a Christian king, is one of the most surprising features of the whole story. The only traitor throughout the long weary siege was a Portuguese gunner who unfortunately got off scot free.

News of the plight of Mombasa had reached Goa in September, and in December a relief fleet of two frigates, *Santo António de Taná* and *Nossa Senhora do Valle*, and two galliots (small transports) set out commanded by General Luis de Mello de Sampaio, a "country-bottled" *fidalgo* of very little experience and of very dubious reputation. He had a double mission. First to relieve Fort Jesus and then to carry trade goods to Moçambique and assume the position of General of the Rivers of the Cuama (Zambezi). This was a fatal order to issue. The first duty was bound to be unremunerative in cash and probably in honour, and the temptation to hasten on to the second would be irresistible. Second-in-command was José Pereira de Brito, a commoner who by efficiency and courage had worked his way up the ladder of promotion. He was to be the hero of the siege and would have been the saviour of the Fort if he had been allowed to do what he wanted. The Captain of the other frigate *Nossa Senhora de Valle* was Henrique Figueiredo de Alarcão, an unenterprising if not cowardly individual. On his way to India the Captain of Moçambique had begged him to take aid to Mombasa but he had refused, making the usual successful excuse that it was not in his *regimentos* or orders. Later he was to abandon his post outside Mombasa and to allow the garrison of the Fort to die of starvation while he enjoyed the hospitality of the Queen of Zanzibar.

It is pathetic that the efforts of man to control the waywardness of man so frequently operate to his own discomfiture. The Portuguese bureaucratic system was particularly vicious in this respect. Although the *regimentos* never seem to have kept an officer on the mark if he wanted to move off it, they succeeded in giving him a perfect excuse if he wished to avoid any obvious and necessary obligation that did not please him. However, the Portuguese in the seventeenth century were not unique. There are parallels in all fields of contemporary life.

The relief fleet floundered across the Indian Ocean, made its landfall on the Horn of Africa and arrived off Mombasa on Christmas Day 1696. It heard the sound of the guns, and the intrepid Barroso came out in an outrigger canoe to ask for immediate help. A ship's boat was sent with fifty men but she grounded beneath an Arab battery, probably below the European Hospital. The soldiers fled towards the fortress. Mogo de Mello sent out some Swahili troops, whom they took for enemies. When they saw them, they ran into the sea and attempted to swim across to the mainland; of the fifty, there were only three survivors. Later operations were more successful. The Venetian captain of one of the galliots, João Francisco, ran her aground beside an outwork without loss, and provisions and munitions were also brought in by the ship's boats during the night.

Towards the end of January, the winds began to change and the two frigates lying off the bar felt their exposed position. A council of war was held. The junior officers wanted to enter the *Barra de Antonio* or Mombasa Harbour and storm the Arab redoubts. Pereira de Brito urged an attack on the Arab vessels in Kilindini Harbour, which he considered would bring the siege to an end. This plan was strongly supported by Mogo de Mello and the Augustinian Prior, the principal Portuguese in the Fort.

However, the pilots declared against entering Mombasa Harbour and the general against attacking Kilindini. He said he was too weak to attack and in any case he had been forbidden to enter Kilindini Harbour. This was false, but he was tired and anxious to get to Moçambique. He considered he had done enough, and after landing some soldiers he left at the end of January. The second frigate was ordered to blockade the port as long as possible and then go to Zanzibar to support the pro-Portuguese faction. Figueiredo de Alarcão did not wait long but soon sailed to Zanzibar, allowing five Arab vessels to enter the harbour. The surviving galliot had secret orders to follow the general. The general in *Santo António de Taná* reached Moçambique safely; the galliot was lost on the way. He sent two small ships with reinforcements and provisions under Rodrigues da Costa but they never got further than Zanzibar. A pinnace with provisions from Damão arrived off Mombasa but finding no warships to escort her joined the other non-cooperators at Zanzibar. By the beginning of July starvation and disease had reduced the Portuguese defenders to the Captain, the Augustinian Prior and two soldiers, and the loyal Swahili to Bwana Daud, a relative of the Sheikh of Faza, his followers and eight Africans, probably about thirty men in all. There were also forty African women who were apparently now living in the Fort and not in the ditch. A Portuguese gunner, Lourenço Nunes, deserted and greatly improved the efficiency of the fire of the Arab batteries.

On July 20, just before dawn, scaling ladders were raised against the walls of the Fort. A sentry gave the alarm and the African women carried a dying Portuguese soldier to a bastion, where he fired the two swivel guns with deadly effect. Bwana Daud and his followers, including the African women, pushed off the ladders and hurled grenades among the Arabs. The attack was broken off. It cost the Arabs eighty dead and many wounded.

The site of the action was at the Flag Bastion, presumably on the eastern flank of S. Mateus. Here the ditch is narrowest and the wall lowest in relation to the top of the counterscarp. The bastion of the swivel guns was probably the south flank of the gun-platform. On the Cienfuegos plan of 1728, the bastion of S. Mateus is called the Baluarte de las Banderas. However, on the Lopez de Sá plan, there is a fine flag flying from the bastion of S. Alberto, and it is possible that the scaling ladders were placed against the middle of the curtain wall between S. Alberto and S. Mateus. The wall here is higher than between S. Mateus and the gun-platform, but it is the second best position from which to storm the Fort if you have to carry out this disagreeable operation. The *Kitab al Zenuj* mentions the west wall of the fortress as the site of the attack but, unless the whole of the wall above the parapet is Arab, this would demand very long ladders.

This was the last battle of Mogo de Mello. The Augustinian Prior and two soldiers died during the next two days. On the 24th the Captain gave orders for his grave to be dug in the chapel and handed over the Fort and a Portuguese boy of eleven to Bwana Daud, enjoining him to remain faithful to the end. Four days later he died. Bwana Daud maintained his charge for six weeks with unflinching loyalty and courage. Resisting equally threats and blandishments he held the Fort with his unsoldierly, mainly female band. Admitting the higher appreciation which personal loyalty enjoyed in those days compared with ours, in which the conception of loyalty has been largely replaced by the democratic sense of solidarity, it is incredible to us living in the twentieth century that he should not have taken the commonsense way and handed over the Fort under conditions of safe-conduct or amnesty for himself and his followers.

Nevertheless, he was saved. The incredible also happened at Moçambique. The general was shamed into returning to Mombasa and after reaching Zanzibar, where he once more wavered, was bullied by Pereira de Brito into going to see what was happening in the Fort. The pilots were even induced to enter Mombasa Harbour, and the frigate and two smaller vessels anchored in front of the Fort. The Arab guns fired on the frigate but no guns fired from the Fort. Rodrigues de Costa ran his galliot aground at the outwork and got into the Fort. At midnight a letter reached the frigate describing the situation, and the next night the general landed. Bwana Daud presented him with the keys of the Fort which he had the grace to hand back to the man who had saved it. The second galliot was also run aground under heavy Arab fire. On October 20, the frigate's cables parted and she grounded opposite an Arab redoubt, north-east of the Fort which was probably on the point below the European Hospital. One large, nine and a half feet long and six and a half inch bore, and two smaller six and a half feet long and three and a half inch bore cannon which probably belonged to this ship were recently brought up by divers. Against his inclinations the general was forced to authorize offensive operations to extricate the crew, and Pereira de Brito carried out a series of sorties which cleared the adjacent redoubts. But the general was ill with fever and on November 19 he died in the Fort. The command devolved on Pereira de Brito, who initiated a policy of aggressive defence although Arab reinforcements had arrived, but the Portuguese were steadily losing men and the outlook, in spite of the two able and energetic commanders, was gloomy. Orders had to be given to forbid statements likely to cause despondency and alarm, and the situation began to assume the same complexion as it had at the end of the previous year.

Alarcão had returned to Goa in the *Nossa Senhora de Valle* in June and reported the serious state of the fortress, but nothing could be done until the return of the Persian Gulf Force. This force arrived in November and in December, with commendable promptitude, went off to relieve the Fort.

The squadron, consisting of two large frigates, one small, and a galliot under the command of General Pereira de Silva, reached Mombasa on December 28 and anchored off the bar. Pereira de Brito urged him to enter Kilindini Harbour and destroy the enemy redoubts, now eight in number. The galliot with provisions should not enter the harbour but could send provisions and munitions to the Fort by ships' boats at night. The customary initial blunder was made and one boat with its complement was lost, but subsequent operations were successful. The general, like his predecessor, Luis Mello de Sampaio, refused point blank to undertake any offensive operations and was gratified when the renegade Nunes, who had returned to the Portuguese, gave support to his reluctance by stating quite falsely that there was a chain across the harbour.

He tried to make Pereira de Brito commander of the fortress but he refused. He then appointed Leandro Barbosa Soutomaior, a disagreeable individual who quarrelled with the loyal Swahili so that they refused to remain in the Fort. Bwana Daud and some of his followers were evacuated to Goa together with the gallant girls; others made their peace with their enemies and went home. The general sailed away on January 18, having spent even less time than Mello de Sampaio at the Fort. However, he did stay at Zanzibar until September and before returning to Goa sent a ship with a few troops to fill the gaps and to swell the ultimate roll of casualties.

Of the events of this last year of the siege we know very little, and even that little reached Goa two years later by word of an Indian who claimed to have been in the Fort when it fell. The end had come on December 13, 1698. On the 12th the garrison was reduced to eight Portuguese, three Indians and two African women. The Captain sent a boy over the walls to get salves for his sores. The boy was captured and told the Arabs the state of affairs. During the night the Arabs scaled the walls at the Flag Bastion and at the gun-platform near the postern gate. The Portuguese withdrew fighting to the cavalier bastion of S. Antonio but at seven in the morning the Captain, weary of the hopeless battle, ran out firing his blunderbuss and was shot down and killed. The soldiers surrendered but two of them blew themselves up with many Arabs in the powder store, where they said gold had been hidden. Either the next day or a week later on December 20, the relief fleet arrived and saw the red flag of Zanzibar flying over the broken battlements. Neither Pereira de Brito nor Bwana Daud were on board so they were spared the sight of the loss of what they had fought so hard to hold. As for the commanders, the useless Alarcão and de Silva, they could not have cared less, and probably murmured a *Te Deum* as they turned their ships into the wind to sail for Zanzibar. It has been estimated the defence cost the Portuguese eight hundred dead, of whom four hundred died in the Fort or in its vicinity, about three thousand Swahili, one frigate and four galliots.

The fact that the Fort survived so long with so little help from outside shows that it could have been held, provided that it was provisioned punctually each year. If the last relief fleet had arrived a week earlier, the Fort would have been relieved and garrisoned, as had happened in 1696 and 1697. If Pereira de Brito and Bwana Daud had been in command, the siege would have been raised once and for all, either when the *Santo António de Taná* came back from Moçambique or when the second relief fleet arrived. The greatest weakness of the Portuguese was their appalling choice of commanders. Besides this major defect, the continual shortage of powder, supplies and men was of minor account. The junior officers showed all the courage of the preceding centuries; it was their superiors who were incapable of any action that was not obviously to their immediate advantage.

The seamanship shown by the Portuguese sailors was deplorable. The reluctance of the pilots to enter either Mombasa or Kilindini Harbour must have made their ancestors of the fifteenth and sixteenth centuries turn in their graves. The irascible Vasco da Gama would have ordered the whipping post to be set up immediately. The handling of the small boats would have shocked any fisherman of Cascais or Setubal into blasphemy. The Arabs were infinitely their superior at sea. Their cutting-out expeditions against the galliots were well planned and resolutely executed. On land they showed themselves miserable soldiers, no match for the disease ridden, half-starved soldiers of the garrison.

The artillery on both sides appears to have had a greater moral than practical effect. Most of the cannon balls found in the Portuguese levels have been small; three and a half inch diameter weighing four pounds for a falconet; and one and a half inch diameter weighing six and a half ounces for a swivel gun. Only two five and a half inch diameter balls weighing twenty pounds have been found. There were also stone balls six inch diameter weighing thirteen pounds, and three and a half inch diameter weighing two pounds. The real justification of cannon seems to have been the chance of a lucky shot; only at sea was it a weapon of decision. On land, it was still the day of the musket, the hand grenade, and cold steel. The Portuguese showed that, when resolutely led, they could still be masters of the battlefield.

9

The Mombasa of the Omanis

THE MOMBASA of the eighteenth century was little less turbulent than it had been in the preceding centuries. A Portuguese intelligence report of 1710 describes the Fort and town, probably the old town of the Moors, as overgrown with bush. It states that the Arab governor was living in the house of Miguel de Faria; that most of the soldiers were in huts in the Rua do Padre Juliares, extending to the cashew nut distillery; that the forts at Makupa and Ras Serani were manned, but only a patrol of five men guarded Fort Jesus at night. This may be true only of the year in which it was written, because in the interval between the fall of the Fort in 1698 and the Portuguese re-occupation of 1728, certain works were undertaken.

The Lopez de Sá plan shows the modifications carried out by the Arabs during the first thirty years of the Arab régime, of which the most important was the digging of a square well behind the cistern. The well is marked on the plan as "made by the Arabs", and the Portuguese are no more likely than anybody else to give credit to others for work done by themselves. The couraça is described as unfinished, which suggests that it is a new Arab couraça that is mentioned and not the couraça of Rezende's description and the Cienfuegos plan. The nicks in the apex of the arches of the gunports are evidence that the present couraça is Arab rather than Portuguese.

A certain disenchantment—to use the modern expression

—had set in. The Omanis were quarrelling with the Mosungalos over their ration of cotton cloth, and arguing with the Mombasans over who was to pay for the soldiers. It was a sensible principle of the Sultans that their African possessions should pay for their own defence. When they demurred, he was willing to discharge the garrison and wait for the inevitable request by somebody for his intervention.

The first governor or governors are not known by name but a certain Sahdad bin Sahdi or Ahmad bin Said, is mentioned who returned to Oman in 1728, leaving Nasir bin Abdulla al Mazrui in his place. The African slave soldiers in the Fort mutinied and chose one of their number called Sese Rumbe as commandant. The Omanis retired to the Augustinian convent which they fortified. The Mombasans refused to recognize the new régime and supported the evicted governor.

The crisis in Mombasa was an opportunity for Bwana Tamu Makuu of Pate to relieve himself of the full weight of the Portuguese expedition which he had invited to come to help him against the Omanis. The rebel soldiers, feeling rather lonely and that they must belong to somebody, had declared their allegiance to him, the nearest they could get to an African, and with his aid the Portuguese were able to recover the Fort and town. On March 16, 1728, High Mass was celebrated in the Fort before a rough wooden cross. The general was another Lúis de Melo de Sampaio, of feeble memory, but the gallant Bwana Daud was also present. The Omani garrison, contrary to the wishes of the Sultan of Pate who wanted them to be killed, were allowed to return to Oman and Sese Rumbe was sent to Moçambique. The Sultan returned to Pate, advising the Portuguese to work the Mombasans like slaves, which apparently they were not loath to do.

The new Captain, Alvaro Caetano de Melo e Castro, was an arrogant and stupid individual who succeeded in quarrelling with his own soldiers as well as with the Mombasans. The order of events is a little confused, but there is no serious contradiction between the Portuguese records and the Swahili histories. In a wave of unseasonable morality the Captain turned out of the Fort all the girls, who had been living with the soldiers and, with equally unseasonable confidence, permitted the stores of husked rice to be taken out to be cleaned. Of course, it was never brought back and when the crash came the Fort was without reserves of food or female company.

Bwana Tamu soon regretted the whole business of bringing back the Portuguese. Although he had given them Fort Jesus, they had insisted on building another fort at Pate. The anti-Portuguese parties in both towns joined forces and an insurrection was planned in Mombasa. It was organized by a Pate adventurer named Manni Hamid, who had come over with the Portuguese and was living in Mombasa. The leading personage in Mombasa was a Sheikh bin Ahmed, the head of the old sheikhly house of Malindi; the Captain had also succeeded in alienating him, and he took part in the conspiracy.

A feast day in April 1729—perhaps Palm Sunday—was chosen for the outbreak and a number of Portuguese outside the Fort, including the small garrison at Makupa, were killed. The remainder were blockaded in the Fort. In November, realizing that an Omani fleet might arrive and that their relations with the Mombasans, on whom they were dependent for food, would be severed, they capitulated. Those that wished were allowed to retire to Moçambique but a certain number stayed behind, became nominal Moslems and presumably married their mistresses. There was always a curious ambivalence of love and hate in the relations of the Portuguese with the Swahili and the Africans. Something of the same nature was observed in German-occupied Europe, though it is only just becoming fashionable to mention it.

Caetano restored the Fort after its thirty years of Arab occupation, but unfortunately no details have been recorded, except that the chapel was intact and had been used as a store. The Lopez de Sá plan of 1728 shows the Fort as it was in this year. The attractive hypothesis that this is a works plan cannot be adopted, as it would hardly show an "unfinished couraça"; nor can it show the work actually carried out by Caetano because Lopez de Sá left in May, only three months after the recovery of the Fort.

The re-occupation of the Fort is described as having been an orderly operation in which each tribe put a man there "so that nothing should be lost". The tribes of Mombasa and the surrounding hinterland in the eighteenth, and probably seventeenth century, were very different from what they had been in the past. The Mosungalos had disappeared or been absorbed into the Nyika; the Mvita had shrunk to a ninth part of the Nine Tribe group, which with the Three Tribe group formed the Twelve Tribes of Mombasa. Relations between tribesmen and townsmen were closer, although there was no question of assimilation. The Nyika tribes made no claim to equality, but expected to be well paid by their nominal masters.

The masters were divided into two groups: the Thalatha Taifa or Three Tribes, and the Tissa Taifa or Nine Tribes. The Thalatha Taifa were the larger in numbers and were led, at the time of the revolt, by the Sheikhs of Malindi, Tangana and Kilindini. Later the Thalatha Taifa are known as the Chamgamwe, Tangana and Kilindini and are generally led by the Sheikh of Malindi and supported by the Nyika. The prestige of the Sheikh of Malindi and Mombasa continued throughout the eighteenth century, and into the nineteenth century. The Sheikh of Owen's day (1823) was a more impressive personality than the Mazrui Governor and nothing was done without his consent. He was also pleased to be regarded as the Portuguese consul and spoke a little Portuguese, an interesting suggestion that the Portuguese had not left too bad an impression. Subsequently, the family seems to have declined and at the time of the collapse of the Mazrui (1837) the leading local dignity was the Sheikh of Kilindini.

The ruined mosque of the Kilindini, also known as the Mosque of the Three Tribes, was built in the eighteenth and rebuilt in the early nineteenth century. The cistern, well and mueddhin steps belong to the original building, but the musalla and qibla are later. An inscription recorded by Guillain, which has now disappeared, gave the date of the completion, probably reconstruction, as Hejira 1221 or A.D. 1808.

The Thalatha Taifa were all Arab-African or Swahili refugee groups from the destroyed Arab settlements of the mainland. In Guillain's day (1846) they were more African than the components of the Tissa Taifa.

The Tissa Taifa consisted of Nine Tribes whose names have varied. The History of Mombasa which was written down in 1823 for Lieut. Emery, does not enumerate them, but Guillain lists them Mvita, Mtwapa, Jomvu, Kilifi, Melinde, Shaka, Faza, Pate, and Gunya. A later list omits Melinde and adds Omwe. The present list omits both Malindi and Omwe and adds Katwa, which is a Swahili term for Somali. Of these only Mvita, the first, is certainly the old mediaeval stock of Mombasa; the Mtwapa and Jomvu may be part of the old set-up; the rest are as much immigrants as the Thalatha Taifa. In spite, or because of their number of units, the Tissa Taifa were generally at a disadvantage compared with the Tissa Thalatha. They are found supporting first the Omani governor against the Sheikh of Malindi, then the Omani murderers of the Omani governor against his brother. Minorities generally prefer foreigners—better a stranger than a step-mother.

The third element, the Nyika tribes known as the Miji Kenda or the Nine "Towns", consisted of Digo, Giriama, Duruma, Kauma, Chonyi, Ribe Jibana and Kambe. In the History of Mombasa four others, subdivisions of the Digo, are also mentioned by name. Their choice of overlords, according to Guillain, is interesting. The Giriama gave their allegiance to the Mvita; Chonyi to Mtwapa; Kauma, Kambe, Ribe to Kilifi; Rabai to Jomvu and Malindi; Digo, Duruma, Jibana to Kilindini. So only one of the Thalatha Taifa and five of the Tissa Taifa had territorial connexions. The delegation which went to Oman to offer allegiance anew included representatives from all these tribes, townsmen and countrymen, Muslim and infidel. There seems to have been no question of Sheikh bin Ahmed being asked to resume the seat of his ancestors.

The first governor was a Muhammad bin al Maamry who governed without incident; but the second, Saleh bin Muhammad al Hadhrami, supported the Tissa Taifa against Sheikh bin Ahmed. Sheikh fled to the Nyika who broke into the old town and plundered it. Later Sheikh and his son Ahmed fell into the hands of the governor and were put to death in the Fort. Subsequently, Saleh was recalled and Muhammad bin Othman al Mazrui was sent in his place.

The vexed question of the pay of the soldiers was settled, according to the Kitab al Zenuj, by the Mazrui agreeing to pay them. However, this was soon a purely academic question. The Yaarubis, who had built up the greatness of Oman, degenerated and were succeeded in 1741 by the Albusaid, but the Mazrui governor of Mombasa declared his independence. The Albusaid were unable to deal with their African possessions until they were finally established in Oman, but they did not forget. In 1746 they sent Seif bin Khalaf and four other assassins, "the five Seifs" (*seif* is the arabic word for sword) to kill the rebel governor. They succeeded in their mission and took the Fort, but the brother of the governor, Ali, was lowered over the walls and escaped. He appealed to a friend, the captain of an English ship from Bombay then in the harbour, named either Kirby or Cook, who told him to make ladders and take the Fort by night attack. This he succeeded in doing with the help of the Nyika, but the assassins held out in one bastion and he again appealed to the obliging Englishman. A cannon was landed from the ship which blew a hole in the bastion and the assassins surrendered and were executed. Ali succeeded his brother and granted fresh privileges to the Thalatha Taifa and the Nyika. The Tissa Taifa of the town who had recognized Khalaf as the new governor were ignored.

Ali bin Othman was an energetic person. He took Pemba from the Sultan of Pate, though later, after Pate forces had landed on Mombasa island and broken into the town, he was obliged to concede half the revenues of the disputed island. Subsequently, he invaded Zanzibar and was on the point of taking the town when he was murdered by a disgruntled nephew. The expedition returned to Mombasa and elected a cousin, Masud bin Nasir (1753-75), who was succeeded by Abdulla bin Muhammad (1775-82).

This was the golden age of the Mazrui in their government of Mombasa, which stretched from Kilifi to Pangani. The centre of Mombasa had moved into the area of the Portuguese town, leaving the old "town of the Moors", the *Mji wa Kale*, to become the shanty town it is today. The wall between the two towns built by the Portuguese was extended on the west on the line of the later Rogers Road and Makadara Road by Ahmad bin Muhammad (1782-1814) and his son Abdulla (1814-23). The side facing the Fort, where there was a wide open space, which became the cemetery of the Mazrui, was left open. Here are buried Muhammad bin Othman, his sons Abdulla bin Muhammad and Ahmed bin Muhammad, and his grandson Abdulla bin Ahmed. In 1823 the wall was hurriedly repaired by Suleiman bin Ali when the Omani threat first became apparent.

The walls have disappeared but an attempt was made by the late Mr. G. Stevens and Mr. A. Hamid of Mombasa Municipality to trace them from local information and the Owen plan. The Owen plan is highly schematized but includes a rectangular projection on the north which must have had some foundation in fact. The present Wall Street is on the line of the stretch of wall on the west side of it, and could have been named for this reason. The main gate was the Kilindini Gate which was near the point where Old Kilindini Road crosses Rogers Road.

The Guillain plan, made twenty-three years later, is less schematic and shows a polygonal north end which fits nicely a line running along the east end of Princess Marie Louise Road, Portuguese Street and the south end of Mzizima Road. Guillain shows the Kilindini Gate and mentions a road leading from a West Gate or Makupa Gate to the fortress. This may be the same as the Kilindini Gate. The east end of the road would have been *Ndia Kuu*, which is clearly directed on the main gate of Fort Jesus. Stevens' plan shows the Kilindini Gate, the *Lango la Kuinama*, a gate at the end of Mzizima Road where it runs into *Ndia Kuu*, and a gate in Fort Jesus Road, opposite the bastion of S. Phelipe between town wall and Fort, but these other gates may not have existed.

During the eighteenth century the condition of the Fort steadily deteriorated until it reached the deplorable state described in Owen in 1824:

> The interior of Mombasa fort is a mass of indiscriminate ruins, huts and hovels, many of them built wherever space could be found, but generally formed from parts of the ruins matted over for roofs. When seized from the Portuguese, every building within the outer wall was thrown down, and the foundations torn up to search for treasure supposed to have been hidden there. The fine tank which once contained water enough for two or three years cannot now be traced without great difficulty.

The reference to the destruction in the Fort, if true, must refer to its fall in 1698. I am inclined, however, to think the story is greatly exaggerated. From the finds in the excavations I should put the collapse of the Portuguese buildings to the end of the eighteenth century. The absence of reference to the chapel shows that it was no longer recognizable.

In the middle of the eighteenth century, an open hall, The House of the Mazrui, was built against the outer wall of the old Captain's house, which was now in ruins. The two doors in the wall were blocked, a new doorway with a round arch was made, and a masonry bench with three attached pillars built along the wall. The outside wall of the hall consisted of a bench between two pillars of the old portico and a large opening for a door at the north end of the wall. The builder must have been an Indian because in each spandrel of the arch of the doorway was a carved marigold boss, which is neither a Portuguese nor an Arab decorative feature. The rolled edge of the bench is also an exotic refinement which I have seen in no other building in East Africa. Against the inner face of the wall was a dais, two sides of which were painted with bands, lozenges and circles in black

16(a) Fort Jesus, Mombasa: Gate, built 1634.

(b) Arms of Mateus Mendez de Vasconcelos, last Captain of Malindi and first Captain of Mombasa.

17(a) Fort Jesus: Chapel, Cistern and Cavalier Bastion. Seventeenth century.
    (b) Fort Jesus: West Parapet Walk. Late sixteenth century.

and red. It would be reasonable to associate this construction with the assumption of independence by the Mazrui in the middle of the eighteenth century. At the end of the eighteenth or the beginning of the nineteenth century, a wall was built over the outer bench and an upper storey was added to the hall, supported on wooden beams with Koranic and religious texts. This was the room where Lieut. Boteler and Captain Vidal were received when the proposal for the treaty was made. The mention of the decorated ceiling would appear to refer to the Koranic inscription carved on the beams, some of which has survived. It is uncertain where the Governor lived; it may have been in the north-west bastion or over the gate-house or in the town. It is strange that neither Owen, Guillain nor Von Decken make any reference to the Governor's house. The question of purdah was raised when Lieut. Reitz expressed the wish to live in the Fort, but this may have been merely an excuse to keep him out of it. At this time also extensive repairs were undertaken to the whole of the gun-platform. The lower line of crenellations, the gunports and the turrets in the outer corners belong to this period. The profile of the seafront is therefore predominately Arab.

On the death of Abdulla bin Muhammad, civil war broke out over the succession. Eventually Ahmad bin Muhammad succeeded and his two rebel brothers were killed by the Nyika. In 1813 he intervened in the Pate succession and the Mombasa forces suffered a disastrous defeat at Lamu. A year later he died and was succeeded by his son Abdulla who defied Seyyid Said, but Mbaruk bin Ahmad, his warlike brother was forced first to withdraw from Pate and then from Pemba. Abdulla died in 1823, and again there was a succession dispute between Mbaruk and Salim, another brother, which was decided by the election of a third party, an uncle called Suleiman bin Ali, a useless old man, deposed in 1825.

At the beginning of 1824, Seyyid Said had begun the campaign against the Mazrui. Threatened by an Omani fleet on February 9, 1824, Suleiman signed the convention

M

with Captain Vidal, putting himself under British protection and accepting a British resident. The first, Lieutenant, lately Midshipman, Reitz died after six months and was succeeded by another ex-Midshipman, Lieutenant Emery. It is interesting that midshipmen were considered in those days the most suitable persons to appoint as governors. They did not do too badly, but the task was impossible. The Protectorate was never ratified and on July 28, 1825, Emery was withdrawn after eighteen months of struggle. The Mazrui considered that they had been promised the restoration of Pemba and resented the measures taken to suppress the slave trade and to protect His Majesty's Indian subjects as well as the collection of customs duties. Emery lived in Leven House, an Arab building on the harbour lent to him by Mbaruk. Later this house was given by Seyyid Said to Dr. Krapf and it remained in the possession of the C.M.S. until 1891, when it was passed into the hands of the Imperial British East Africa Company. It was pulled down early in the twentieth century. The site is near the end of the Leven Steps and has been absorbed into the customs establishment. Emery constructed the flight of steps and the jetty outside the house. He also constructed the first customs house wharf, a watering place and a well beside it. The flight of steps, the passage through the rock leading down to it and the well survive as monuments to a very remarkable officer; many of the stones came from the Portuguese forts at Ras Serani.

Sir John Gray in his excellent book on the Protectorate is a little hard on Emery. A more experienced man would have done nothing and become a cipher. It should be remembered that his job involved the continual interference in what the Mazrui considered the rights of government. With the little support he had, he could only win respect by acting autocratically, as if the British Navy was always just over the horizon. It is incredible that he got his way so often. British officers in those days did what they thought was right, or was in accordance with their orders, and frequently succeeded. To behave in this irresponsible way now would be quite intolerable. Anyway, he had demonstrated for the first time in East Africa that the ruling class was subject to the law as much as anybody else. It made a bad impression on the Mazrui but it may have made the Mombasans think. With the departure of Emery, the slave trade was resumed. Several French ships took on their cargoes or, in the eighteenth-century parlance, "slaved" at Mombasa. However, Seyyid Said's operations were also resumed; on January 4, 1826 he arrived in person. The battery at Ras Serani, now known as Fort St. Joseph, had been repaired, but the Mazrui were in no sense able to compete with the guns of the Omani fleet, nor were they willing to face the losses and discomforts of blockade. Negotiations ensued and Seyyid Said got possession of the Fort, though Salim remained as governor living in the town. In 1828 Nasir bin Suleiman, Governor of Pemba, arrived to replace him. Salim refused to be replaced and Nasir was besieged in the Fort by the Mazrui and the Mombasans. At the end of the year he was forced by starvation to surrender and on the appearance of an Omani fleet in 1829 was put to death, probably in the Fort. It was not until 1834 that Seyyid Said was able to resume serious operations against Mombasa but these were unsuccessful. The main feature was the setting up of a battery at English Point or more likely Mackenzie Point, on the opposite mainland, to bombard the Fort with mortar bombs. These were large hollow cannon balls and have appeared in the excavations. They are a useful control on the dating of the levels in which they are found.

The Fort having been repaired since Emery's day was able to return the Omani fire, and eventually operations were broken off. During the siege Sheikh Salim is said to have struck a small copper coin the size of a sixpence, the value of a *kibaba* of maize, from a Portuguese cannon in the Fort. There are coins in the British Museum with the word Mombasa on one side and on the other *dhurab*, meaning "struck". A similar coin exists with the name Lamu which suggests that these coins belong to an earlier occasion.

The Mazrui had won again, but this was their last success. Sheikh Salim died in 1835, his colourful brother Mbaruk was also dead, and a younger brother Muhammad, the hope of the house, had been killed in an attack on the Omani battery. After some unsavoury intrigues, a certain Rashid bin Ali was recognized with reservations by some other members of the family. However, among the Mombasans there was already a pro-Omani or defeatist element. The Sheikh of Mtwapa, Mwenge Kombo, was put into Fort Jesus where he died. A late pillar tomb in Kilifi section of the *Mji wa Kale* is said to belong to a Sheikh Jabir who was part of the anti-Mazrui party. When Mwalim bin Shafei, Sheikh of Kilindini, the most important person in Mombasa after the Mazrui Governor, went over to Seyyid Said there was nothing to be done. In 1837 Rashid surrendered the Fort, which was immediately garrisoned with Baluchi and Omani soldiers. Subsequently Rashid and some twenty-five to thirty leading Mazrui were invited to pay their respects to Seyyid Khalid, the son of the Sultan, in the Fort where they were arrested and deported. Some of them were thrown overboard on their way to Bunder Abbas, others died of starvation in prison. Nasir bin Suleiman was avenged and Seyyid Said was at last master of the coast. Seyyid Said was a great and kindly ruler. I doubt if he was ever troubled by a thought of his treatment of the Mazrui. The fact that they had died of starvation in his prison did not mean that their blood was on his head. "Thou shalt not kill but need not strive officiously to keep alive" is an English witticism but it should have been written by the Arab. The English in their unregenerate days were not unduly reluctant to shed blood.

The surviving members of the family fled to Takaungu and Gazi, where they were allowed to remain unmolested. The Takaungu Mazrui accepted philosophically their change of fortune, but the hatred of the Gazi Mazrui endured throughout the century, bursting into flame, and then dying down to smoulder uneasily.

The change of government made no immediate changes either in Mombasa or in the Fort. In 1846 Guillain describes the inside of the Fort as being full of huts, as it was in Owen's day. He mentions the broken battlements and dismantled batteries, and states that the only surviving Portuguese buildings were the galleries in S. Matias which were used as powder magazines. The town of Mombasa he describes in the following uncomplimentary words:

> One part of the town is made up of blocks of stone houses with a single story and a balcony, the other of veritable hovels with only a ground floor and a thatched roof, like those in Zanzibar. Except for a long road leading from the fortress to the west gate or Makupa Gate, the blocks of houses are very irregularly divided by narrow lanes constantly changing their direction, a true labyrinth in which a stranger could not find his way without a guide. Gavana does not possess a single building worth mentioning.

Guillain mentions the ruins of three Portuguese churches. Part of the Augustinian Convent had been converted into a house for the Qadhi; the small Misericordia church was the home of the family of Suleiman bin Ali, and the third, presumably the old Parish Church where Reitz was buried, was being used as a cow byre by a Banian. He estimated the population at three thousand Swahili and their slaves, two hundred and fifty Arabs and fifty Banians.

The first known commandant or Akida was Abdulla bin Mbaruk al Bakshwein. He was succeeded about 1845 by the Baluchi Jemadar Tanggai bin Shambe—Guillain calls him "poor Tanggai", one of the most shameless scroungers who ever flourished in East Africa.

Fifteen years later, there were two more literary visitors: the German Baron von Decken and an Englishman Richard Thornton, whose unpublished diary has been brought to my attention by the kindness of Mr. H. A. Fosbrooke. Thornton describes the court as full of huts and mentions only two buildings of stone, one presumably the house at the east end of the court, the other the cavalier bastion in the north-west corner. He says, however, that building materials were being collected. One of the buildings put up at this time was the house in the south-west bastion, later demolished, which could be dated by the European porcelain found below the floor. Much of it came from the Utzchneider factory at Sarrguemines which was founded about 1858. Tanggai was still Akida but much older and unable to exort so much from the learned baron as from the equally erudite French captain. A man who had the stamina to spend the evening arguing with Rebmann† over sins of necessity was not the type to be bamboozled by an ageing jemadar.

Tanggai was succeeded by Muhammad bin Abdulla, son of the preceding Akida. Muhammad bin Abdulla was an ambitious, unbalanced and not over-clever servant of the Sultan. He fought the rebel Mbaruk with fair success but quarrelled with most of the Mombasans. Finally, in desperation, he refused to obey his order of recall and attacked the Governor and the loyalists in the town. Sultan Barghash appealed to the British and on January 18, 1875 two men-of-war, the *Nassau* and the *Rifleman*, bombarded the Fort with cannon and rockets for two hours. A shell from a six and a half ton gun hit the turret in the angle of the gun-platform facing the north and brought it down "with the matchlock men inside it". Muhammad bin Abdulla was treated with customary leniency. Later he went to Madagascar and married Birira-Vun, Sultana of Bisina, whose domains he put in order. Eventually he returned to Zanzibar and died in 1894, curiously enough still anxious to return to Mombasa, the scene of his downfall.

Along the stretch of coast south of Mombasa there were a number of small settlements, represented today by the ruins of humble mosques and occasional tombs. This is an area that was not occupied by the Galla, though Vanga was sacked by them in the eighteenth century. Near the Tanganyika border is the site of Umba or Vumba Kuu, a small state usually hostile to Mombasa. Off the coast opposite Shimoni is the island and anchorage of Wasin which is shown on Dalrymple charts and had a certain nautical importance. The passage from Shimoni was used frequently for the crossing to Pemba when it belonged to Mombasa.

The oldest of the existing ruins is probably the inland

† A German missionary, the companion and successor of Krapf.

mosque of Muunge, built on a plinth above the low lying land around the settlement. Over the qibla is a frieze of bowls, reminiscent of the qibla at Chwaka in Pemba. The other mosque on the shore is similar to the mosque at Diani and to several others in Tanga area. They all have plain qiblas, anterooms on both sides made by walls pierced with pointed arches but no pillars. The mosque at the mouth of the Tiwi River, known as Kongo, has a vaulted roof and has been rebuilt. None of these mosques except Muunge, I think, is older than the eighteenth century.

The walls of Vumba have mostly fallen into the ravine of the Vumba river, but it may once have been more important than it appears today. There was a history of Vumba which has been lost, but some details have survived, mainly dealing with the relations of the Diwani or ruler with the Digo and Segeju in the seventeenth or eighteenth century. There are also references in Portuguese sources to a Diwani Mwana Chamby Chande who was ruling about 1659, and another Mwana Chamba in 1728. Vumba was abandoned in the eighteenth century as a result of Galla raids and the population moved to Wasin island. Later some of them returned to the mainland and settled at Shimoni and Vanga.

In the middle of the nineteenth century, the most important place was Gazi where one branch of the Mazrui had established themselves after the débâcle of 1837. Mbaruk bin Rashid was the last fighting Mazrui. From 1872 until 1895, when he was driven over the border into German territory by the forces of the new Protectorate, he was in open or covert rebellion against the Sultan. In 1871 he sacked Vanga but was subsequently defeated in an attack on Likoni on the southern mainland opposite Mombasa. He then retired to his stronghold at Mwele on the edge of the Shimba hills. This was his hideout in times of emergency, although he was never able to hold it. It was taken in 1872 by the Akida and again in 1885, and in 1895 by the Sultan's forces backed by naval parties. His rebellion took the form of raids for cattle and slaves which he sold to the Sultan's other subjects in Pemba.

The war between Sir Arthur Hardinge, the British Consul-General in Zanzibar, and Sheikh Mbaruk in 1895 was a gentlemanly business so far as the leaders were concerned. Marches and counter-marches were punctuated by exchanges of letters regretting the differences that had arisen between them. These had naturally no effect on the regard which the two gentlemen had for each other. Grotesque and quite undemocratic; we should do things very differently today, and provide employment for numbers of people who would otherwise find it difficult to make both ends meet. The most prominent supporters of Mbaruk was Khamis bin Kombo, Sheikh of Mtwapa, an irreconcilable upholder of the old feudal régime. He was put into Fort Jesus like his ancestor, though unlike him he did not die in the Fort but was allowed to go to Tanganyika.

To the north of Gazi, near the civil hospital at Msambweni, is an enclosure backing on the sea with a room over the gate known as Tumbu which was probably a slave pen owned by Sheikh Mbaruk. Here we have the less gentlemanly side of one of the gentlemen.

10

Zanzibar and Pemba

ZANZIBAR AND PEMBA are the largest of the many
islands off the coast of East Africa. Most of the west coast
of both islands enjoys a rainfall and an abundance of water
that is the envy of the opposite mainland. They are, of
course, not as lush or as odiferous as the west coast of Ceylon
or the islands of Indonesia, but the tropical fruits which are
the delight of these countries can be grown with success.
The east coast is East African in character and marginal
in the opprobious sense of the word. The Portuguese General,
Francisco de Barreto, described Zanzibar in 1571 as the
finest part of East Africa.

It is possible that Zanzibar is mentioned in the *Periplus*
and by Ptolemy, though the island of Menouthias is as likely
to be Mafia, in spite of the views of Captain Guillain in favour
of Zanzibar. However, Zanzibar and Pemba would have
been among the first places to be settled by Arab or Arab-
African immigrants south of Somalia. After the expulsion
of the Portuguese they formed part of the overseas dominions
of the Sultan of Oman, and later constituted the Sultanate of
Zanzibar. Up to this time they had been independent of
each other. Zanzibar was very early associated with Kilwa
and Mafia; Pemba with the mainland opposite, as well as
with Mombasa and Pate. It is significant that the small copper
coins of Kilwa and Zanzibar are rare in Pemba and none
was found in the excavations at Ras Mkumbuu, showing the
different economic systems of the two islands.

169

The population of both islands claims or claimed to be Afro-Shirazi, that is, to be related to a greater or less degree with Persia. What they say now that Zanzibar is independent is uncertain; popular racial origins are apt to change with political attachments, but the language of both is closer to the Segua of the mainland than other Bantu groups and has certainly no connexion with the language of Omar Khayyam. In the eighteenth and nineteenth centuries, there arrived an Omani aristocracy who later developed the clove plantations which are the main source of wealth of the islands. Capital came partly from the profits of the mainland trade in slaves and ivory, and partly from loans from Indians. The oldest established Indian families of the coast are to be found in Zanzibar, but very few are likely to be older than the nineteenth century.

The medieval Sultan of Zanzibar is said to have been a scion of the royal house of Kilwa, and the connexion between the two settlements is shown by the participation of the rulers of Zanzibar in the affairs of Kilwa and the resemblance of the coins of the two cities. The study of the coins of East Africa has only just commenced, but from hoards found in Zanzibar it would appear that the two important rulers were a Husain ibn Ahmad and an Ishaq bin Hasan, both ruling in the fifteenth century. The Kilwa history mentions a Hasan bin Abu Bekr, who may have been the father of the Ishaq of the coins.

The Portuguese attacked Zanzibar in 1503 and again in 1509 and destroyed the principal town, which may have been on the site of the present Zanzibar. Subsequently relations improved; the Zanzibaris took part in the destruction of Mombasa in 1528, and did not participate in the hostilities of 1586 and 1589, or the revolt of Dom Jeronimo in 1631. There were Portuguese settlers, a church and an Augustinian priest who were no great credit to the Portuguese, according to the judge Pedro Alvares Pereira. After the revolt of Dom Jeronimo the settlers, or some of them, were removed to Mombasa, but the lessening of contacts did not produce an improvement of relations. In 1654 Cabreira in his second tour of office was forced to carry out a punitive expedition, in the course of which the town was destroyed and the queen expelled.

This unsuccessful rebellion had been promoted by the rising power of Oman, and the swift retribution was sufficient to ensure the loyalty of Zanzibar for the rest of the century. During the long siege of Fort Jesus, the greatest friend of the besieged—their own countrymen not excepted—was Queen Fatima of Zanzibar, who sent supplies to the beleaguered fortress and harboured the relief ships when they were unable or unwilling to go to Mombasa. She paid for her partisanship by the destruction of her town, and when the Fort fell was exiled to Muscat. She was eventually allowed to return home, and her son Hasan to inherit the title of ruler, though it is unlikely that he had any more power than Mwenye Mkuu of the nineteenth century. In the eighteenth century Zanzibar maintained her tradition of what some would call spiritless loyalty, this time to the Omani governor, and what is more, influenced him in the same direction. When the ruling family of Oman changed from the Yaarubi to the Albusaid, Zanzibar alone of the East African dependencies remained faithful to the new Sultan.

In the nineteenth century she had her reward, though to what extent the pre-Omani Arabs or Swahili benefited is uncertain. Seyyid Said, the able and fortunate Sultan of Muscat, made his East African dominions his main interest, and Zanzibar entered on a golden age which was to continue through the lives of Seyyid Said and his four sons Majid (1856–70), Barghash (1870–88), Khalifa 1 (1888–90) and Ali (1890–93). During this period the whole commerce of East Africa, import and export, passed through the hands of the merchants of Zanzibar. This came to an end in 1895 with the building of the railway from Mombasa to Kampala and the creation of the ports of Mombasa and Dar es Salaam, which has left Zanzibar with only her cloves and coconuts and a certain tourist potential.

The present town of Zanzibar is certainly on the site of the town of the seventeenth century, as the church is embedded in the wall of the fort, but there is a case for Unguja Kuu as the town that was burnt by Ravasco and Duarte in 1503 and 1509. Outside the Beit al Ajaib are three fine early sixteenth-century Portuguese guns counter-marked with Arabic inscriptions: these were lost at the fall of Ormuz, taken by the Imam of Muscat from the Persians and finally brought to Zanzibar by Seyyid Said.

The Beit al Ajaib, the Palace of Wonders, was built by Seyyid Barghash in 1883 as a ceremonial palace on the site of the old town house of Seyyid Said. Its greatest attraction is the series of carved doors which are among the finest examples of this art.

In the country there are a number of ruined palaces of the Omani period in which the most striking features are the harem baths. They can be seen at Marahubi and at Chuk-wani and Kedichi; the baths at Kedichi are the best pre-served. The only palace of historical interest is Seyyid Said's country residence at Mtoni. The two upper floors have been removed, but the ground floor has survived in good con-dition. It was here that he received with charm, dignity and penetration the fantastic creatures that his European contacts had brought into his life; the Englishmen Owen, Livingstone, Burton, Speke, the Frenchman Guillain, the American Waters, in addition to many other minor eccen-trics of the nineteenth century. I do not include the remark-able Hamerton, the British (né Irish) Consul who was to become almost part of his own character. The two were not parted for long; Seyyid Said died at sea on October 19, 1856 and Atkins Hamerton on July 5, 1857 at Zanzibar.

Another monument in a different vein is the lugubrious slave pit on the lonely beach at Mangapwani where slaves were penned waiting shipment. Towards the end of the trade a scoundrelly Commissioner of Police was convicted and severely punished for having organized a shipment, probably from this very spot. Whatever private thoughts the Albusaid may have had, they did their duty when it was pressed on them, rather like an English magistrate today punishing an offence against parking regulations. The

172

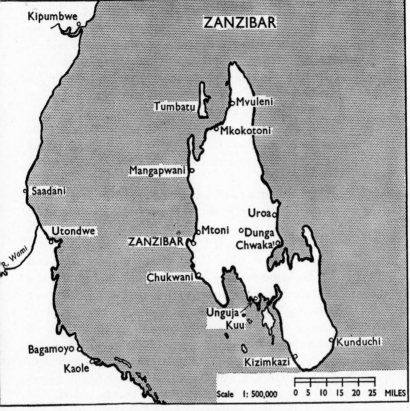

Fig. 12. *Zanzibar*

English magistrate, however, does not enjoy the convicted man's possessions and in fact gets nothing out of it except a scar on his conscience.

Outside the Museum is a series of Indian tombs of the early nineteenth century which are interesting by reason of the variety of decorative patterns.

The town as seen today is late nineteenth century and presents an attractive picture of opulent, static and benevolent imperialism: the direction of the world had been entrusted to the British upper classes; so long as God willed, they would be there; they would always win in the end, and they were generally right; work with them and you would

173

enjoy the benefit of utterly disinterested advice, which you would never get from your friends and relatives, and make a lot of money. Seyyid Barghash had fought them in 1850 and had been blown out of the Palace; Seyyid Khalid his son had done the same in 1895 and met the same fate. They had abolished the slave trade but the clove plantations were still worked, and one was relieved of a lot of troublesome responsibilities. Now God no longer has any interest in the British upper classes and of course things are much more dynamic and better.†

The original centres of Zanzibar island seem to have been on the west coast, in the north at Tumbatu and in the south at Kizimkazi. The old name of the island was Unguja. A site now abandoned, covered partly with bush and partly with coconut palms, is called Unguja Kuu (Old Unguja), and is believed by some to have been the original home of the people who made themselves masters of the island and later founded the town of Zanzibar. The date of the unification of the island is unknown, but the Portuguese do not refer to more than a single ruler. There seems to have been an independent ruler in the north at Tumbatu but he succeeded in avoiding the interest of history. In the centre of the island are the ruins of a large house known as Dunga, which was the home of the last representative of the old rulers the Mwenye Mkuu, whose position but not authority was recognized by the Omani Sultan. It is said to be haunted by the spirits of his murdered dependants.

The most interesting site is on the island of Tumbatu, a quarter of a mile from the mainland at Mkokotoni. The thirteenth-century Arab geographer Yakuti states that the inhabitants left the main island after a hostile attack by their neighbours, and that they continued to live on Tumbatu, although there was no water and they were dependent on a well on the opposite shore. The same state of affairs prevails to this day; the people of Tumbatu have to send over to

† Following the *coup d'état* of January 11, 1964, four thousand Arabs are credibly reported to have been raped, flogged or murdered. What could be more dynamic?

Mkokotoni for water every day. They are a determinedly suspicious people and prefer to have as little to do as possible with foreigners, by whom they mean everyone not a Tumbatu. A harmless linguist was regarded with great dislike because they thought he was associated with a scheme to give them a public lavatory, which they rightly believed was a most sinister form of official infiltration. The majority of the houses are at the south-west corner, as far as possible from outside contacts, but there is a ruined mosque on the shore opposite Mkokotoni. It is an extremely interesting building with a secondary qibla, consisting of a niche in the thickness of the wall in the east anteroom. This anteroom may have been the mosque for women for, although Arab women in East Africa do not now go to the mosque, it is possible that they did in the past. The ablutions were at the west end and are greatly dilapidated. The principal qibla has disappeared and there are no other architectural details.

Six miles beyond Mkokotoni, at a place called Mvuleni, are two ruined houses, said to be Portuguese, which means that nobody knows anything about them. The more interesting of the two buildings is surrounded by a high wall and inside the enclosure is a cave with a well. The other is better preserved and is not far from the shore.

Kizimkazi at the other end of Zanzibar island has or had the distinction of possessing the oldest historical fact in East Africa—the excavation of the Husuni Kubwa at Kilwa may have down-graded it. In the mosque is a dedication inscription with the date 500 Hejira or A.D. 1107. The inscription runs around the north wall and qibla. On the right it consists of chapter ix, 18 of the Koran, followed by xvii, 80–82 round the qibla, and on the left wall the dedication which may be read

> The high and very great Shaikh es-Saiyid Abu Imran Musa, son of el-Hasan, son of Muhammad . . . . . . may Allah grant him long life and destroy his enemies—ordered the building of this mosque on a Sunday of the month Dhu-lqa'da in the year five hundred.

In one of the rosettes in the spandrels of the arch is the beginning of the first words of the Koran xiii, 24; the other is undecipherable. The plaited Kufic with its floreate background points to the east rather than the west, but there are no close parallels and the presence of this elaborate example of calligraphy at the end of the world is a mystery. Saiyid Abu Imran Musa is unknown in history and also to local tradition, but he was no doubt the ruler of this part of Zanzibar. The mosque was restored or rather rebuilt, according to an inscription on the left side of the qibla, in Hejira 1184 or A.D. 1770 and the qibla and trefoil panel ornament belong to this date.

In 1960, in connexion with the restoration of the roof of the mosque, excavations were carried out by Neville Chittick in the mosque and outside the qibla. The excavations revealed the floor of an earlier mosque and the earlier qibla. They also showed that the original mosque had been built on a plinth some feet above the original surface of the ground. There was only one earlier level and it would appear that the site had been abandoned between the two occupations.

Outside the mosque are a number of ornamental eighteenth-century tombs. There are no inscriptions but they are traditionally ascribed to a Sharif Abdulla, a Mfalme Kisa and a Mfalme Ali. The reason for the existence of the mosque and settlement is a small inlet, protected by a headland from the south-west monsoon, which is now used as a haven for fishing boats. At the back of the bay is a sandy flat surrounded by a coral outcrop, crowned for most of its length by a wall. In the middle are the ruins of a house which were excavated at the same time as the mosque was examined. In the sand below the foundations of the house were found early *sgraffiato*, similar to the scanty finds from the mosque area. The perimeter wall was never finished and it may have been begun from fear of the Sakalava of Madagascar, who were raiding the coast of East Africa in the early nineteenth century, then abandoned when the danger had passed.

Beyond Kizimkazi is a village called Kunduchi where in the past was performed a dance with trident fish spears, which is interesting as it seems to have no known affinities on the coast.

18(a) Qibla and Entrance to Minaret of Mosque, Ras Mkumbuu, Pemba. Fifteenth century.

(b) Qibla of Mosque, Chambani, Pemba. Eighteenth century.

19(a) Qibla of Great Mosque, Chwaka, Pemba. Fifteenth century.
(b) Qibla of Mosque, Shengeju, Pemba. Fifteenth century.

There are no monuments on the east coast, but there have been a number of surprising finds which show at least that the world was looking in, if not staying for long. Sir John Gray has pointed out that although this coast has no conventional harbour, there are a number of anchorages, sheltered at times, which would be acceptable to small ships.

Two hoards of coins have been found: one, half a mile inland from Kunduchi, of 176 or more Chinese cash dating from the seventh to the end of the thirteenth century; the other of about 2000 coins of Kilwa and Zanzibar at Uroa on the north side of Chwaka Bay. Another odd find was made at Uroa two years ago: a stone with an inscription in bold Roman letters, clearly of Portuguese origin. The stone is now in the Zanzibar Museum. It is more likely to have been in transit and to have been cast on the shore when the ships in which it was being carried was wrecked. The stone is broken but has clearly marked the words "LEITAO" .... (capi) TAO MOR MENDES. The only "Leitao" prominent in East Africa was Pedro Leitao de Gamboa, the Captain of Mombasa, murdered by Dom Jeronimo. Is this his tombstone that was being sent out from Portugal?

Odd Chinese cash have turned up in excavations at Gedi and Ungwana, and are found from time to time in Mafia and Tanganyika, but the Zanzibar hoard is unique. Chinese cash were at one time exported from China, presumably as metal, but later the export was prohibited because a copper famine was feared. The latest cash known to me is early Ming and was found at Gedi in an early sixteenth-century context.

Pemba, "the Sultan's Other Island", is smaller than Zanzibar but no less fertile, and its Arab name al Khudhra, "the Green Island", is an indication of the impression it made on the first visitors from abroad. In spite of its natural agricultural riches and the number of minor historic monuments, it is almost completely ignored by the historians and geographers before the arrival of the Portuguese. It has, so far as we know, no history of its own; its history was made by others, and its rulers and inhabitants suffered from successive exactions of one or other of its neighbours. It had relations with the mainland and the Queen of Pemba and her son, the King of Otondo, probably Utondwe near Saadani, are mentioned in the second Cabreira expedition.

One of the earliest references to Pemba is in a Portuguese document of 1506 in which it is described as a place of provision for all the large ships of Mombasa and Malindi and having four or five "quarrelling kings". The kings seem to have diminished during the succeeding century, but it remained the source of provisions for Mombasa, and even at times for Moçambique. Where these kings lived is uncertain and the Portuguese references are curiously barren of place names. The largest surviving historical monuments are at Ras Mkumbuu on the west, and Chwaka and Pujini on the east coast. The almost completely demolished site of Mkia wa Ngombe, "The Cow's Tail", on a bluff also on the west coast may have been once an important centre.

During the sixteenth century there were a number of Portuguese settlers in Pemba whose knaveries were so blatant that they became proverbial. One of the minor iniquities which has been remembered was the rule that if a chicken ran or was induced to run into a Portuguese compound, it was acquired by the owner of the house on the grounds that it was a Christian convert. There were no doubt far graver causes for dislike and it is possible that the small sites on the east coast are due to the flight of the population to the less accessible part of the island. The islanders had their revenge at the time of the first Turkish raid of 1585, and the Portuguese were either killed or driven out, together with the king who had become a Christian and had taken the name of Dom Felipe. This no doubt caused joy in Goa and Lisbon, but it was an embarrassment in Mombasa where the best chances of indirect rule were imperilled. A curious Swahili document has survived in Pemba describing the efforts of the Portuguese under "Jojone the Frank" to collect tribute. The first and last Jojone mentioned in the story is certainly the energetic Cabreira, who as a young man of twenty-seven "plagued" the people of Pemba in 1634. He returned in 1654 and they failed to recognize him as the same Jojone. However, when they saw his ring, they accepted the inevitable and paid up.

However, it was not only the Portuguese who had eyes on Pemba. The new Sultan of Mombasa claimed the island, and in 1605 or 1606 took it with his own forces. His successor Hasan was finally recognized as ruler of Pemba in exchange for an annual tribute of rice to the Captain of Mombasa, and the son of Dom Felipe, Dom Estefan, was overlooked. The overlordship of Pemba lapsed after the fall of Dom Jeronimo but was revived by the Mazrui Governors. They exercised authority over the island throughout most of the eighteenth century, although they were forced to share the customs with the Sultans of Pate. The interest of Pate in Pemba is first mentioned in connexion with the treaty of 1728 with the Portuguese in which the claim of Pate to a part of the island is recognized. The same Swahili document mentions a "plantation" of the island by Shirazis and Nabahani conducted by Jojone the Frank. It is possible that the Nabahans were the Nabahani of Pate and the Pate claim was reinforced or even established by this operation. In 1822 Pemba was taken from the Mazrui by Seyyid Said's Governor of Zanzibar and attempts to retake it were all defeated. The operations were a lively memory twenty years later and are described by Guillain.

The only site where there have been excavations is Ras Mkumbuu on the offside of the long promontory which forms the north arm of Chake Creek. I thought at the time that the name Mkumbuu might be assimilated with Kanbalu, the important town mentioned by Masudi in the tenth century, but excavations proved me wrong about the tenth century but not the name. In the Shumofsky edition of the Roteiro of Ahmad ibn Majid, the famous pilot of Vasco da Gama, Kanbalu is shown on an Arab map as an island off the coast of Pemba. The fact that Mkumbuu is an island connected only with the rest of Pemba by sandy flats I was to discover by being forced to wade home about two miles after a Sunday ill-spent in surveying, during which I had not noticed the advance of the tide.

The ruins consist of a large, exceptionally well-built mosque with three rows of rectangular pillars, an arched qibla with a nick at the apex, and on the left a square doorway leading into a round tower, which I believe was a minaret. To the left again was the door for the Imam (Plate 18a). There was no sign of a minbar on the right, which must have been of wood. The mosque is close to the present shore which is becoming overgrown with mangroves, and it is clear that the town once extended much further northwards over land now covered by the sea. Besides the mosque there is a group of square pillar tombs, one of which has a curious decoration at the top, reminiscent of a north African minaret. Only two houses have survived in any state of completeness and there was only time to clear them sufficiently to get the ground plan. One, the House of the Tombs, had two rooms; the other was rather larger with the characteristic three-room plan of the mainland.

The finds were few and consisted of celadon and white porcelain, which I should date not earlier than the fourteenth century. It would appear that Mkumbuu was not the success it was hoped and that it was not occupied for more than a hundred and fifty years. Its remote position at the end of the six-mile-long promontory indicates that it was an alien site with very little interest in Pemba—a ship anchored off a foreign coast, demanding and getting little more than protection from wind and weather. A trial excavation at the top of a hill a quarter of a mile to the east of the ruins produced *sgraffiato* of the thirteenth or twelfth century and there may have been an earlier settlement.

Further up the creek and nearer Chake is a village, Ndagoni, built on a hill which may not be entirely natural. It is a more promising site for a settlement than Mkumbuu and it is possible that the Roman coins in the Zanzibar Museum said to have come from Ndagoni, were found here and not at Mkumbuu, as has always been assumed.

At the end of the creek is Chake Chake, which can be translated, "To each his own"—a very unfashionable attitude today but once quite respectable. It is built on a hill

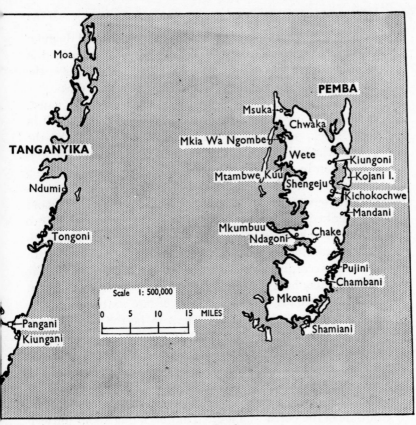

FIG. 13. *Pemba*

with a steep slope down to the creek. There is no old mosque
at Chake but there is a small fort which was once larger and
is said to be Portuguese. This is most unlikely as it is never
mentioned in the Portuguese documents. It was probably
built by the Mazrui in the eighteenth century, when Chake
became the most important town on the island.

The site of the Portuguese settlement is unknown. The only
account of a land operation in Pemba is of the raid of Duarte
de Lemos in 1520. The Sheikh had fled to Mombasa and the
Portuguese, after wandering through the island in search of
cattle, came upon a fortified dwelling where the Sheikh
had kept his treasury. As Barros remarks smugly, "Our

181

soldiers and sailors found some property which paid them for the trouble of the journey." This site has been identified as Pujini which is situated at one of the narrowest parts of the Island, and is clearly more of a unit than a normal town.

Pujini has been cleared but has not yet been excavated. It is unlike any other structure on the island, or indeed in East Africa, and could not have been constructed by the people who built the other settlements on the coast. There is a tradition in Zanzibar, Pemba and the mainland opposite, of people called the Wadiba and Wadabuli, who were aliens and masters and more efficient than the *indigènes*, to whom are ascribed many of the ruins of the coast. Diba is the Arab name for the Maldives which are populated by an Arab-Indian stock. They were primitive enough in the fourteenth century, according to the account of Ibn Batuta, but in the fifteenth may have acquired more of the civilization of India. The surface finds at Pujini consist of late sixteenth-century Ming blue-and-white, which seems to be the date of final occupation.

It is a rectangular enclosure about two acres in extent, with a wide parapet walk running round the top of the walls. Near the north-east corner is a well and on the side of it a bas relief with a horn; in the centre are a number of houses. On the outside of the north wall a ditch has been dug about thirteen feet wide which may have been filled with water at high tide before the silting of the creek. The only local tradition about Pujini which has survived is that it was built by a gentleman called Mkame Mdume "The Milker of Men", because of the high output he demanded of his slaves and subjects.

The third major site is Chwaka at the north-east end of the island, which was in the eighteenth century a residence of the Mazrui governors from Mombasa. Chwaka is built on rising ground sloping down to the mangrove-fringed coast. However, the site is earlier than the time of the Mazrui. The Great Mosque, has an elaborate qibla once ornamented by a row of bowls, and stiff, carved coral ornaments in the form of sunflowers, which are reminiscent of the panels on the inside of the small tomb at Malindi dated to the early fifteenth century (Plate 19*a*). On each side of the qibla are niches, a common feature of Pemba mosques which is not often found in Kenya. The small mosque has plastered domes and a plain qibla, and is probably the mosque built by the Mazrui Governor, Mbarak bin Rashid, who died in 1806. The third monument, Haruni's Tomb, has a pillar in the middle of the east face and crude rounded niches below it. On the inner wall was a relief of a horn and a circle with six segments, which I am informed some local moran has defaced. The horn relief links it with Pujini and there is a local tradition that it is the tomb of a gentleman called Mvunja Pau, "The Breaker of Sticks", who was the son of the Milker of Men—a chip of the old block. In the Pemba document a Nabahani "king" Haruni and his wife Mwana wa Taka (Chwaka) are mentioned; he may be the Haruni buried in the tomb.

The minor historical monuments of Pemba which I have seen are all mosques, and are almost all on the east side of the island. They fall into two groups based on the form of the qibla façades. One of these, including Shengeju (Plate 19*b*) and Shamiani, I believe is fifteenth or sixteenth century. The other, including Msuka, Kiungoni, Mandani, Chambani (Plate 18*b*) and Kichokochwe, is seventeenth, eighteenth and even nineteenth century. Of the latter group Msuka is certainly the earliest and Kichokochwe the latest; with all of them is an absence of order in the design of the qibla, which I would associate with a break in tradition following the upheavals of the seventeenth century.

One other site in Pemba must be mentioned, Mtambwe Kuu on the small island opposite Wete. There are no surviving structures, but the odd finds that have been picked up on the shore indicate that it must be one of the earliest sites on the coast. They have included gold beads and Chinese porcelain with the ogee shaped lotus petal carved on the outside which even I am prepared to concede is Sung and possibly twelfth century. The site is unfortunately partly occupied by the village and by a coconut plantation, but there are open spaces including a mound, either a rubbish heap or a ruined building, which could be excavated.

Pemba has another reminder of the past in the bull fights or bull games, said to have been introduced by the Portuguese, but possibly connected with a similar sport which was in vogue in some parts of Madagascar. They became so popular that they survived the expulsion of the hated foreigners. Whether the bull enjoys it as much as the spectators is a matter of opinion. However, it is not a bloody business; the bull is not harmed and the human participants get the worst of it, which no one can really mind. It compares favourably with most recreations in which *homo sapiens* is brought into contact with his fellow mammals.

Pemba is also noted for its witchcraft, though the recorded instances have not been very impressive. It is said that witch-doctors of all types went to Pemba for post-graduate courses to perfect the arts learnt in the local schools on the mainland. Whether this is correct or not is uncertain. Witchcraft is a profession that does not believe in undue publicity or grant degrees or fellowships. One's merit is measured by what one makes out of it, and at least one witchdoctor on the coast of Kenya does very well with only his local training.

II

Tanganyika

We know very little about the mainland of Tanganyika with the exception of the Kilwa area, both before and even after the arrival of the Portuguese. The settlements on the northern part of the coast do not appear to have been as large or as important as those in Kenya. The domestic buildings, partly as a result of the nineteenth-century commercial activities, do not seem to have survived, as at Gedi and Ungwana. The Portuguese were concerned with Kilwa in their early days, but after the withdrawal of the garrison in 1512 had very little to do with this part of the coast. There were settlers from time to time at Tanga, Kwale near Kisiju, and Mafia but nothing is heard of them, except when they were murdered. The Bantu tribes appear to have been long established and their movements were oscillations rather than migrations, such as the southern flight of the Nyika. The only major upheaval was the march of the cannibal Zimba from Kilwa to Mombasa 1586–89, which must have devastated the coastal territories. Kilwa, of course, is another question but her political influence did not extend beyond Zanzibar and rarely beyond Mafia.

The activities of Seyyid Said and the Omanis had a greater impact on Tanganyika than any other part of the coast. Armed with English and American muskets, the Arab trading expeditions pressed further and further into Africa in search of ivory and slaves. The decayed Arab settlements on the coast awoke to a new life and their influence was projected

185

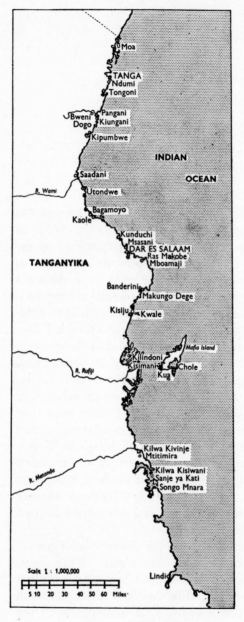

across Africa. The most important of these were Bagamoyo and Kilwa Kivinje but there were others, many built on old abandoned sites, to confuse the archaeologist with an illogical mixture of *sgraffiato*, celadon, willow-pattern and bottle glass.

The nineteenth century was the "Indian Summer" of the Arabs of East Africa; never had they enjoyed such prosperity and security. The slave trade was admittedly no longer the simple business it had been, and was clearly a dwindling asset now that the accursed English had taken it into their heads to interfere, but they paid well for ivory and gums, and there was money to be made in guns and

FIG. 14. *Tanganyika*

alcohol. The whole coast, with the exception for a short time of the stretch between Vanga and Pangani, was clearly in the hands of the Sultan, and his authority was increasingly marked along the trade routes that ran up to the great lakes and beyond. The shock of the German ultimatum delivered in 1885, and what can only be described as the British betrayal, was all the greater, since this was the area of the coast where the Sultan was a greater presence than in Kenya and Somalia.

The centres of the new régime were Bagamoyo, Tanga and Kilwa Kivinje. At Bagamoyo a Governor's residence was built which has survived as an impressive example of "Colonial Imperial". I have never heard of ghost stories about the *Residenz* but it is easy to imagine the spiked helmets, the swords and the moustaches—all the pomp of yesterday, only fifty years distant in time and yet as remote as the echo of the guns of Vasco da Gama. Later, the capital was moved to Dar-es-Salaam which had been founded some twenty years before by Seyyid Majid and then neglected by his successor Seyyid Barghash. Under the British Mandate the capital remained at Dar-es-Salaam though during its last years there was some talk of taking it up-country. The independent government has decided to stay on the coast, which from the point of view of those who like antiquities is to be welcomed. It is always difficult to assure yourself of the importance and attraction of things you will seldom have an opportunity to enjoy.

The three provinces into which the coast of Tanganyika is divided, Tanga, Eastern and Southern, are convenient divisions for the three main groups of monuments and have indeed historical precedent. The most important of the northern sites is Tongoni, the centre of the old state of Mtangata. The ruins consist of a mosque and a large group of pillar tombs dating from the fourteenth and fifteenth centuries. The clearance of the mosque and the excavations carried out by the Department of Antiquities in 1958 indicated that the settlement was not earlier than the fourteenth or fifteenth century, and that it had probably been abandoned and reoccupied in the eighteenth or nineteenth century. The mosque is exceptionally large and elaborate and is of Chittick's northern type, with the musalla or place of prayer separated from the ribati or anterooms on east and west side by walls with arched doorways (Fig. 1a). On the west is an extra room and at the south end a long room running across the back of the musalla and the two rooms on the west. Near the mosque are the tombs, some contemporary and some eighteenth or nineteenth century. Three of the tombs had square pillars, four had octagons. One of the square pillars has survived and was mentioned by Burton. The settlement has disappeared.

The ruler of Mtangata was normally hostile to Mombasa and therefore friendly with the Portuguese. A lapse from loyalty occurred in 1631 when the Portuguese settlers were murdered at the instigation of Dom Jeronimo. There was still a ruler in 1728, as he is mentioned as having returned to his obedience, but some time later there may have been a shift of population which would account for the break in tradition and the virtual desertion of Tongoni.

There is an interesting small mosque at Ndumi not far from Tongoni in the middle of a walled enclosure. These walled villages are to be found in the Tanga area. Most of them were built for defence against the Masai by the Segeju, the descendants of the tribe which destroyed the cannibals outside Malindi. The Segeju were unable to stand up to the Galla, and after making a long inward sweep returned to the coast down the Umba valley. They are mentioned as a distinct group by Krapf but are now largely merged into the surrounding population. The best preserved of these fortified enclosures is Kigirini. Ndumi is somewhat different and is probably early eighteenth century. The projecting angle covering the gatehouse is reminiscent of the inner wall of Gedi, built at the end of the sixteenth century.

Pangani at the mouth of the Pangani River one would suppose to have been an important centre but, apart from two large, rather grotesque tombs with oval tombstones at Bweni Dogo across the river, nothing has survived to suggest it. The present district centre is built on an alluvial flat and there may be an earlier site higher up the river. The area was developed by German sisal planters and if there was anything of interest it is surprising that nothing has turned up. On the headland south of the Pagani River, known as Kiungani, is a fine pillar tomb with a doorway in the southeast corner.

On Toten Island in Tanga Harbour are two ruined mosques of the eighteenth or nineteenth century. Medieval sherds have also been found there, showing that there was an earlier settlement.

The eastern, actually the central province of the coast, lies opposite the southern end of Zanzibar and the Mafia group of islands. It can be equated with the state of Otondo, mentioned by the Portuguese, whose name may have survived in the village of Utondwe not far from Saadani. Like Mtangata, Otondo or rather Utondwe was normally hostile to Mombasa in the sixteenth century. After the revolt of 1631 it was made tributary, and later in 1654 was punished by Cabreira for intriguing with the Omanis. The son of the Queen of Zanzibar, Fatima, was Hasan the ruler of Otondo who later succeeded his mother in Zanzibar. No ruins have survived of the towns of the state of Otondo unless it included Kaole, the Pambuji of the Portuguese and the predecessor of the caravan terminal of Bagamoyo, four miles away.

Kaole is built on a low-lying stretch of ground near the mouth of the creek. The monuments include two mosques, a group of pillar tombs and some ruined houses, and the town must once have covered a considerable area. Excavations were carried out in 1958 and 1959 by the Department of Antiquities. The large mosque (Fig. 1b) has a plain qibla without any decorative features and two anterooms, one of which is carried round the south end as at Tongoni. The washing arrangements are also at the south and include an interesting *birika* or cistern with pointed arches and a roof consisting of twin barrel vaults. Against the north wall is built an extremely tall pillar tomb with two illegible inscriptions. The other mosque is smaller but with a decorated pillar and is of the "southern" type, with two rows of pillars and no anterooms (Fig. 1e). One of the houses was cleared and its plan was found to resemble the houses at Gedi. Finds from below the floor of the mosque suggested a date in the thirteenth or fourteenth century for the foundation of the settlement which, from the absence of sixteenth-century porcelain, was probably abandoned in the fifteenth century. The fact that the Portuguese only once mentioned Pambuji suggests that by the sixteenth century it had ceased to be of any consequence.

At Kunduchi is a ruined mosque with a collapsed qibla, once ornamented with roundels, which is probably fifteenth century. At two other sites, Banderini and Makungo Dogo, are two small mosques in recognizable condition. The more interesting of the two is at Makungo Dogo with an ornamented west door. However, most of the surviving buildings on the stretch of coast south of Bagamoyo are eighteenth and nineteenth century. Of this period are the pillar tombs at Msasani and the mosque at Mboamaji with its transverse arches. The date over the entrance 1017 (A.D. 1608–09) must be a stone reset from an older mosque on the same site. The written word, even inscribed on stone, cannot necessarily be depended on any more than that written on paper.

On the other hand, evidence of very early settlement on this part of the coast is now coming to light. Ras Makobe on the south mainland opposite Dar-es-Salaam, and Kisiju, half way to the Rufiji River, have produced *sgraffiato* of the twelfth or thirteenth century. Somewhere in the Kisiju area may be the great mart of Rhaptum of the *Periplus*.

Off the south end of the province and opposite the mouth of the Rufiji is the island group known as Mafia. Mafia is said to have been conquered by the son of the first Sultan of Kilwa who later succeeded him, and relations with Kilwa always remained close. In fact, until recently more coins of Kilwa had been found at Mafia than on Kilwa itself. The Portuguese had an agent at Mafia and a small blockhouse which has not yet been found. The inhabitants are known as Wambwera and are related to the people of the mainland opposite. The distinguished Sharifian family of the Shatry have large properties in Mafia. It is one of the pleasantest places in East Africa, spared by the difficulty of communication, except by air, from the ills that accompany all forms of development.

The principal island was known until recently as Chole or Chole Shamba, to distinguish it from Chole Mjini, a small island off the north-east corner which was the nineteenth- and twentieth-century centre. The present district headquarters is Kilindoni on the west side of the island, opposite the old Kisimani Mafia, from which the group takes its name.

Kisimani Mafia was built on a low-lying stretch of ground opposite the mouth of the Rufiji where a sand spit offered protection from the south-west monsoon. Large quantities of *sgraffiato* and Kilwa coins have been found on the beach where the old site is being eroded by the sea. Excavations carried out in 1957 uncovered a mosque with a series of five floors, dating from the end of the thirteenth to the end of the fifteenth century. From the scarcity of later finds, it was probably at its height in the fourteenth century and then decayed, possibly as a result of the encroachment of the sea due to tidal changes. Where the population went is unknown. Their interests may have been as much on the mainland as on the island and they may have swelled the settlements around the later Dar-es-Salaam. They are unlikely to have gone to Kua, the other and larger site on Juani Island, on the east coast near Chole. A history of Mafia has survived which mentions the hostility between the two towns ending in the ruin of both. Students of European history of the twentieth century know how easily this could happen.

Kua is a large site of about thirty acres with a palace, at least five mosques and a large number of houses. All these buildings, except for one mosque, belong to the eighteenth century when Kua must have been a place of considerable local importance. Just as Gedi is a type town site of the fifteenth century, so Kua is a similar type site of the eighteenth century. It has been cleared and planned but there have been no excavations. Chance finds have shown that there are earlier levels and it may even be contemporary with Kisimani. The palace (Fig. 15) is an interesting well-preserved building, quite unlike the other palaces at Gedi, Pate, Kilwa or Songo Mnara. Kua was destroyed in the early eighteenth century by Sakalava raiders from the west coast of Madagascar. The surviving inhabitants then moved to Chole where they felt more secure.

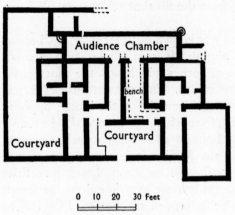

FIG. 15. *Plan of palace at Kua*
(*By courtesy of the Department of Antiquities of Tanganyika Govt.*)

Chole was largely rebuilt by the Germans when they made it an administrative headquarters. The site was ill-chosen because of the badness of the harbour, and a move was being considered. It was not, in fact, carried out until the time of the British Mandate. Today the rows of empty shops and houses, now covered in bush, and the broad *Hauptstrasse*, are a reminder that "dead and done with" is not always a comfortable several-hundred-years-ago.

Some miles to the south of the Rufiji River is the boundary of the Southern Province in which are the remains of the great city of Kilwa, that at one time represented East Africa in the eyes of the western world.

The Kilwa archipelago, consisting of the islands of Kilwa, Songo Mnara, and Sanje ya Kati, form a group of old settlements similar to the Lamu-Pate group in Kenya. Kilwa attained fame and fortune before Pate and, from the surviving remains, enjoyed a rather higher culture. After all, the colonials of Kilwa, whether or not they were of princely stock and whatever they were to be later, had come from a city of luxury and taste, Shiraz, and not from a shabby port

20(a) Domes of Great Mosque, Kilwa. Fifteenth century.
  (b) Court in Husuni Kubwa, Kilwa. Early thirteenth century.

21(*a*) The Gereza, Kilwa. Eighteenth century.
(*b*) The Palace, Kilwa. Eighteenth century.

on a barren coast in which the only achievement could be the making of money. Today there is not much to choose between them in standard of living, though the inhabitants of Pate, through their tobacco cultivation in the ruins, are considerably better off financially. Kilwa has, however, a tourist potential which, when the present admirably executed excavations are completed, will make it one of the most interesting historical sites along the whole coast of Africa. It is hoped that the independent government of Tanganyika will build and back an unpretentious hotel on the island.

Kilwa shares with Pate the distinction of a history which has survived in three versions Portuguese, Arabic and Swahili. These were the languages spoken on the coast of East Africa in the sixteenth century, but only the Portuguese version is contemporary.

The foundation of Kilwa is ascribed to the tenth century by the Arabic version and to the eleventh century by the Portuguese, when Ali bin Husain or Hassan, a son of a sultan of Shiraz by an Ethiopian mother, emigrated to Africa with his family to escape the disparagement of his mother's slave origin. Both the tradition and the date offer considerable difficulties which the archaeological evidence has emphasized rather than dispelled.

Ali's regal birth is very much a matter of doubt. The history of Shiraz is well authenticated, but it has been impossible to find a Sultan Husain or Hassan. The noble pedigree of the Sultans of Kilwa may well be a myth invented later to add lustre to the dynasty. The problem of the date of the foundation of Kilwa is more important. The Portuguese and Arab sources commence and end in reasonable agreement, but in the middle of the Arab version is an apparent lacuna of about one hundred and fifty years, which includes any reference to the establishment of the gold trade with Sofala and the domination of Kilwa over Mafia and Zanzibar. The chronology is based on names of sultans and their regnal years, and there may be duplications of one and extensions of the other. Counting back from the earliest corroborated ruler, the Mudhaffar Hassan visited by Ibn

N

Batuta in 1332, and eliminating all the sultans in the Portuguese list, of whom nothing is recorded except the length of their reigns, an initial date is reached at the beginning of the twelfth century, which is archaeologically acceptable. An even more drastic operation would eliminate another Daud and another Hassan and put this date forward to the middle of the twelfth century. This, however, would shorten too much the time left for the recovery of Kilwa after the Shanga occupation. At the present time there is no conclusive fact to decide whether the tradition or either of the two alternatives is nearer the truth.

The new "state" rapidly spread up the coast and took in the island of Mafia, but on Songo Mnara or Sanje ya Kati there were old Arab-African settlers who disliked the intruders, and who could probably justify their dislike by the fact that the newcomers were heretic Shia Muslims while they were orthodox Sunni. At the beginning of the eleventh century the old settlers were able to drive out the Shirazis and for a short time to appoint a puppet ruler of their own. The rightful ruler Hassan bin Suleiman I, no. 5 in the list, 1005–42, finally returned and the usurper was killed. This was the last kick of the unregenerate past and Kilwa was free to follow her destiny without the threat of a hostile neighbour. This destiny was slow in coming and only began with the capture of the gold trade of Sofala from Mogadishu in the early twelfth century.

The first great king of Kilwa was Suleiman Hassan bin Daud (mid-thirteenth century) who is said to have ruled over Zanzibar and Pemba as well as a large part of the mainland. At the end of the thirteenth century, there was a change of dynasty, but not necessarily a change of family. Freeman-Grenville suggests that the new Sultan was a relative on the female side and a foreigner. There is later evidence of the maintenance of contact with members of the family who had remained in Persia. The new Sultan Hassan bin Talut, 1277–94, is described as a horseman, and as such he would have been an exotic type on the tropical coast of Africa. He also introduced a coinage of small copper tokens, possibly

worth a kibaba of grain, a common measure in Arab countries. They were struck by many of his successors and also by
the rulers of Zanzibar, but were probably never an indis-
pensable factor in the trade of the coast. It is possible also
that at this time Kilwa became orthodox Sunni.

His grandson, Hassan bin Suleiman III (1310–33),
the Abu Mudhaffar Hassan of Ibn Batuta, has attained a
fame which he deserved far less than his predecessors. Abu
Mudhaffar seems to have been a miracle of fatuous piety and
futile generosity. The Great Mosque remained in ruins and
he left an empty treasury to his brother and successor. Ibn
Batuta, who was always an interested party in any matter
of generosity or hospitality says:—"When the virtuous and
liberal Sultan died—may the mercy of God be upon him—
his brother Daud became king, and conducted himself in the
opposite manner. When a poor man came to him he said:
'The Giver of Gifts is dead, and has left nothing to give'."
It was probably no more than the truth. This is the period
when Pate claims to have conquered the whole coast and
there may be something in the claim, although the history
of Kilwa ignores anything so discreditable.

However, Kilwa was in decline, and perhaps suffering
depopulation. An important event, perhaps the most important, since the acquisition of the gold trade of Sofala is
recorded in the Swahili version. In the translation of Freeman-Grenville:—

> Then came Wamalindi from their home, Malindi. They
> went to Sultan Mohamed and greeted him. Then the Sultan
> said to the Wamalindi; "Settle here at Kisiwani". The
> Wamalindi answered: "If we settle here, what shall we
> receive?" The Sultan answered: "Settle here with me, and
> you and you will receive the office of amir and the office of
> qadhi". The Wamalindi agreed and settled at Kisiwani.

If this Sultan Mohamed is Muhammad bin Suleiman
(1412–21), real power in Kilwa had passed to Malindi
immigrants in the fifteenth century, since the offices of
Qadhi and Amir were the most important in the state.
Sultan Muhammad, known as "The New Rain", by

this bold merger had hoped to restore the falling fortunes of his country. He may have stemmed the rot. His son Suleiman bin Muhammad (1421–42), was at least able to restore the Great Mosque, but otherwise the history of Kilwa in the fifteenth century with its thirteen sultans is a depressing story of futile rivalries. On three occasions, the Amirs attempted to take the show as well as the substance, but legitimist sentiment was too strong for them and they were later obliged to put up members of the royal house. One feels that neither winner nor loser had any intention of doing anything with the power to which they aspired. Kilwa still enjoyed control of the gold trade through her governors at Moçambique and Sofala, but the miserable intrigue of her citizens when she had to face the Portuguese peril showed that there was not much sense left in them.

The end came on July 23, 1505. The soldiers of Francisco d'Almeida landed, the Sultan fled and the town and palace were taken and sacked with no excuse and very little opposition. A fort was built on the harbour for a Portuguese garrison, but the Portuguese soon found the site unhealthy, the problem of supply so difficult, and the station so commercially unprofitable that they withdrew.

In the second half of the eighteenth century there was a certain revival of prosperity due to the development of the slave trade. This had always been a second string to the bow of Kilwa, and it acquired a new importance with the European demand for slaves for America and the French islands of Mauritius and Reunion. A French *entrepreneur*, M. Morice, strongly recommended that there should be a French Protectorate over Kilwa but his government, anxious to find allies against the British in the Indian Ocean, did not wish to quarrel with the Sultan of Oman. The Sultan of Kilwa was quickly reminded of his obligations to his suzerain by the Governor of Zanzibar, and a garrison was sent to live in the castle on the harbour to see that he did not forget.

The monuments of Kilwa are principally public buildings (Fig. 16). They consist of three castles (Husuni Kubwa, Husuni Ndogo and the Gereza), the Palace, the Great

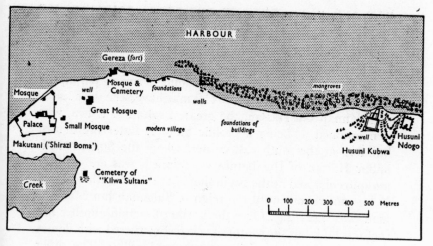

FIG. 16. *Map of Kilwa*

Mosque, the Domed Mosque, the Malindi Mosque, and the Mosque on the Wall. There are no pillar tombs—an interesting fact which seems to confirm the story that the ruling class came direct from the Muslim world, and that the pillar tombs are a local product, not an importation. There are two groups of tombs, one the eighteenth-century tombs beside the Malindi mosque; the other, some of which may be earlier, near the creek next to the Palace, which are traditionally the Tombs of the Sultans.

Excavations at Kilwa were begun in 1958 and are in progress. The two oldest and most important buildings in their present state are the Husuni Kubwa and the Great Mosque. The Great Mosque, with its eighteen cupolas and eighteen barrel vaults, is the finest medieval mosque in East Africa (Plate 20a and Fig. 1f). It consists of two parts: a northern section containing the qibla which had a flat roof, and a southern with cupolas and barrel vaults. Neville Chittick, who is carrying out the excavations, has made the following reconstruction of the history of the site, with which I agree.

The earliest part of the mosque consists of the northern section with the ablutions on the west and the vaulted passage on the east. This was probably covered by a flat roof

197

carried on wooden pillars. It may be as early as the twelfth century. Subsequently, the east and west walls of the old mosque were doubled and the mosque extended southwards by a number of monolithic columns forming perhaps a cloister around an open court. This may have been the mosque of Sulaiman bin Hassan, the greatest sultan of Kilwa, who is mentioned as being a prolific builder. Later the domed building at the south east corner, where the Sultan Mud-haffar Hassan of Ibn Batuta worshipped, was added. The mosque collapsed at the beginning of the fourteenth century. It was not rebuilt until the reign of Suleiman bin Muhammad (A.D. 1421–44). Over the northern section another flat roof was laid, but the southern was reconstructed with domes and barrel vaults carried on octagonal pillars. The qibla and most of the north wall also dates from this period of the final reconstruction. This was the building seen by the Portuguese which the impressionable German, Hans Meyer, compared to the Great Mosque of Cordova. The southern section overlaps the northern by one bay on the east and two on the west. Communication between the two sections was through the third and fourth bays; the third bay is now blocked by a crudely built qibla. Beyond the south wall are the tanks for washing before prayers, and a house with a rather odd plan, perhaps for the Imam or Khatib. A little way from the mosque on the west is a well with a remarkable vaulted chamber about nine feet from the top. The date of the collapse of the mosque is uncertain but the excavator believes that the south wall gave way early in the sixteenth century.

A few hundred yards to the west of the Great Mosque is a small domed mosque of nine bays, with an anteroom on the east and south sides, and a tank for washing at the south-west corner. The compartments of the roof are diversified with barrel vaults and plain and fluted domes. The qibla, two vaults and the dome of the central aisle were decorated with blue glazed earthenware bowls, probably fifteenth-century Persian. Above the central aisle is a pillar as at Takwa, which I believe shows that it was a funeral mosque.

198

It would appear to be of the same period as the final restoration of the Great Mosque.

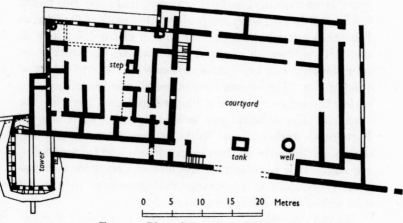

FIG. 17. *Plan of the palace at Kilwa*

To the west again is the Palace, a double-storied building with doors opening into a courtyard with the royal residence on the west and a double series of rooms on the north and south (Plate 21*b* and Fig. 17). At the south-west corner is a rectangular tower with strongly "battered" walls. This building is of more than one period but none of it is older than the eighteenth century. A Sultan Yusuf bin Sultan Hasan of the time of Morice (A.D. 1776–84) is recorded as having done some building with the profits of the slave trade. The Palace is set in the middle of a walled enclosure of about five acres with one side running along the shore. In this wall is a small mosque with a qibla, plundered of its bowls, and the usual anterooms on east and south. Opposite on the landward side looking over a small creek is a tower, and there are other remains of buildings including a rather plain mosque, probably all belonging to the period of modest revival in the eighteenth century.

On the other side of the town towards the open sea is the *Gereza* or Fort, (Plate 21*a*) built on a coral ridge projecting into the sea. It is certainly on the site of the Portuguese fort of Santiago which was completed in three weeks, but to what extent the present building can be regarded as Portuguese is uncertain. The later features, including the rooms inside and the entrance, are probably the work of the famous Ethiopian eunuch Yakuti, who was in charge of Kilwa in the early nineteenth century. The date on the inscription over the gate has been read variously as the equivalent of 1789 or 1807. The broken circular north-east tower shows an earlier square corner with a blocked gun port covering the entrance. The solidity and strength of the walls suggest Portuguese rather than Arab construction though the details, particularly the battlement finials and the spy holes, are Arab. It is possible that the fort was built by a Portuguese renegade, but it is strange that there is no mention of it by any of the Portuguese sources.

The old town of Kilwa was also in this area but all that has survived is the Malindi mosque and the neighbouring tombs. The qibla is eighteenth but the mosque in its original form is fifteenth century. The most interesting of the tombs is a confection with five arches and a roof consisting of two cupolas with a small pillar between them.

About a mile from the Gereza are two structures: Husuni Kubwa (Plate 20b) and Husuni Ndogo, which are the most interesting and impressive buildings that have so far been uncovered in East Africa. Neville Chittick has not yet published his report and it is for him to be the first to tell the story. However, it would not be unethical to give a brief account of what is to be seen today.

Husuni Kubwa is built on a promontory about fifty feet above the sea level, and is protected on three sides by steep slopes. It covers an area of about an acre. The buildings at present excavated consist of a series of open courts and an octagonal pool and three residences, two back to back, of the normal East African type. At the base of the roughly triangular plan is a large court with long chambers along the sides and twenty-six small sunken rooms behind them, used as stores. It is unlike anything else on the coast of East Africa and would appear to reflect a different way of living. It is the only building which can be seen as an approach to *la dolce vita*. Fragments of an inscription with the name al Malik al Mansur Hassan bin Sulaiman were found. The excavator dates it to the early fourteenth century which suggests that the Hassan bin Sulaiman was the host of Ibn Batuta. Alternatively, with a telescope chronology, he may be the Hassan bin Sulaiman who was driven out by the people of Shanga which would put back the date to the middle of the thirteenth century.

Husuni Ndogo is a square enclosure with towers at regular intervals round the sides, on an adjacent cliff separated from Husuni Kubwa by a gully. There are no surviving buildings inside and no evidence that there were any structures of importance. It would appear to be contemporary and it has been suggested that it was a mosque. If so, it must be the single surviving example of the courtyard type in East Africa.

Inside the bay in which is situated the island of Kilwa is another island called Songo Mnara or Songo Runga. Here are the remains of a large palace and a number of large houses, which are probably fourteenth and fifteenth century. Among the many rooms is a chamber with a high barrel vault, the largest I have seen in East Africa, studded with glazed earthenware fourteenth- or fifteenth-century blue bowls. Near the Palace, probably part of the same complex, is a small mosque with an attractive fluted qibla recess (Plate 22).

There is another mosque known as the Nabahani mosque, perhaps evidence of the conquest of Kilwa in the fourteenth century claimed by the Pate history. Burton describes it as having a qibla covered with blue Persian glaze. This has now disappeared. A curious structure is the building marked on the eighteenth-century maps as a "pagoda". It is surrounded on three sides by mangroves which have grown up with the erosion of the surrounding land. The building itself is on a plinth and so survived. It is probably the *Mnara* from which the island takes its present name, but whether it is a tomb, pavilion or watchtower is uncertain.

There have been no excavations at Songo Mnara and the

sherds that have been found are similar to those from all sites in East Africa, that is, they consist of Chinese celadon and blue-and-white and Islamic glazed earthenware, ranging from the fourteenth to sixteenth century. The Palace suggests to me a greater luxury than is to be seen at Gedi, Pate, Kua or Kilwa. It is difficult to explain this difference from the historical records, which show themselves even more capricious in what they include or omit than is usually the case. The silence of the history of Kilwa suggests that the builder of Songo Mnara could have been no Kilwa monarch. When the Palace is cleared and excavated perhaps we shall find some clues to the mystery.

On another small island, Sanje ya Kati, are ruins of buildings with coursed masonry. Coursed masonry is extremely rare in East Africa but is found in the lowest courses of the Great Mosque and some other buildings at Kilwa. Excavations by Neville Chittick have confirmed the early date of Sanje ya Kati, which would appear to have been the Shanga which was the great enemy of Kilwa in the early days.

On the mainland north of Kilwa there is an interesting site, Mtitimira, south of Kilwa Kivinje. It has walls of roughly squared coursed blocks, which is most unusual. *Sgraffiato* and celadon have been found in the ruins, so it is an early settlement. The mosque is much later and the site was reoccupied, like so many Tanganyika sites, in the eighteenth or nineteenth centuries. Kilwa Kivinje may be the Maghamghub mentioned in the history, where a displaced sultan set up a small dynasty of his own. Its old name was Makongeni, not very different in sound. It became an important centre of the slave trade of the late eighteenth and early nineteenth century. Later it was the administrative centre, only recently transferred to Kilwa Masoko opposite the island.

South of Kilwa there would appear to be few remains earlier than the nineteenth century. The most interesting site is Mgao Mwanga which has a polylobed arch inside the qibla of the mosque. This is the Mongallou of the late eighteenth and early nineteenth centuries, then an important trading station, with "particularly fine blacks".

12

The Comoros, Madagascar and Moçambique

IT WOULD appear that the Arab settlements beyond Kilwa
were neither as prosperous nor as developed as those in the
north. The towns of Moçambique, Angoche, Quiliman and
Sofala remained merely the advanced bases of Arab commerce.

The Comoro Islands consist of Great Comoro or Anga-
zidja, Maiotte, Moheli and Anjouan or Johanna. They are
certainly the Zaledj of Idrisi, and less certainly the Kanbalu
of Masudi. They were originally peopled by the same stock
as the inhabitants of Madagascar, but received strong Arab
influences in the succeeding centuries. The immigrants from
the Persian Gulf who came to Kilwa also settled in the
Comoros, and from the Comoros were founded the Arab
settlements on the north-west coast of Madagascar. The
mixed but predominately Arab population of these towns is
known as Antalaot by the Malagasies, which is also the name
for the Comorans. The Comoros in the seventeenth and
eighteenth centuries, like Madagascar, were a source of
supply for all and sundry, and were presumably paid at
times by their varied customers of every nation and trade:
Dutch, English, French, pirate, government, chartered company. At the end of the eighteenth and in the early nineteenth
century they were regularly and pitilessly plundered by the
Betsimaraka and Sakalava of Madagascar. Every four years
there was a "cropping" of the products of the islands—
women, children and cattle; the men were usually killed.

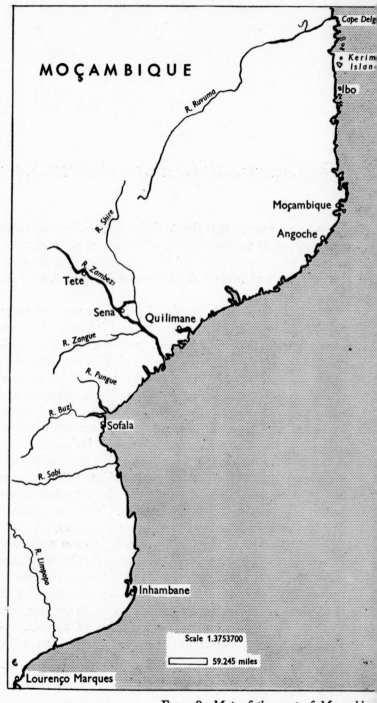

MOÇAMBIQUE

Cape Delg
Kerim
Islan
Ibo

R. Ruvuma

Moçambique

Angoche

R. Shire

R. Zambezi
Tete
Sena
Quilimane

R. Zangue

R. Pungue

R. Buzi
Sofala

R. Sabi

R. Limpopo

Inhambane

Scale 1.3753700

59.245 miles

Lourenço Marques

FIG. 18. *Map of the coast of Moçambiqu*

gazidja

Comoro Islands

Anjouan

Moheli

Maiotte

Nosy Bé

Iharana

Vohémar

Sada

Mahilaka

IHARANA

Nosy Manja
(Old Messelage)

Bembatooka Bay

Majunga

Bueni (New Messelage)

Bali

Antongil
Bay

SAKALAVA

St.
Marie

BETSIMARAKA

Tamatave

Sahadia

IMERINA
Tananarive

BARA

M
A
D
A
G
A
S
C
A
R

ANTEMORO

Matitana

Augustin's Bay

Tulear

Saint
Luces

F. Dauphin

Cape S. Marie

moro Islands and Madagascar

The conquests of Radama the great king of the Imerina and his treaty with Farquar, the British Governor of Mauritius, put an end to these operations. So far as I am aware no buildings have survived. It is possible that there were never towns of consequence. The Comorans do not seem to have attained the sense of community that leads to the wish to spend surplus capital on communal amenities, or the confidence in each other to build walls which must be defended together.

Madagascar and the Comoros enjoy the distinction of having no prehistory or prehistorians and to have been untouched by human or proto-human hand until the arrival of the Indonesians in their outrigger canoes, sometime between the fourth and eighth centuries of the Christian era. These people, the ancestors of the present Malagasies, had come from Indonesia, probably from south Borneo, since the language of Madagascar is closer to southern Minyan than any other Malayan dialect. They were not the most advanced of Indonesians but they had a knowledge of iron working, ceramics and weaving. They had been living for many generations on the mainland, and may have acquired the indubitable African elements in Malagasy culture before their arrival on the island.

However, there were sufficient Indonesian women with them to ensure the survival of the Indonesian language. African women no doubt existed in the colonial *ménage* but they were not an essential part of it, as they were in the Arabic colonial régime. They were forced to learn the language of their masters and their children spoke the language of their fathers. The Indonesians were a megalithic people and the standing stones and square tombs of dry stone masonry are in the megalithic tradition, though few, if any, are likely to go back to the dark ages of the colonization of the great island.

The newcomers spread themselves thinly around their enormous discovery and were followed by other colonists. These included three main groups: their cousins, the Antalaots from the Comoros who had become largely Arabized; pure Africans from the mainland, the Sakalava and the Bara;

and a semi-Islamized Arab-African people, the Iharana. The Antalaots founded a series of towns in the harbours of the north-west of which the most important were Mahilaka, Nosy Manja or Langani, Old Messelage, and New Messelage or Bueni. The ruins of Nosy Manja resemble the other Arab-African towns of the coast and some are certainly as late as the sixteenth century. Nosy Manja was sacked by Nuno da Cunha in 1507 but was rebuilt and only abandoned at the end of the century, as a result of an attack by the Sakalava. The survivors moved to New Messelage in Bueni Bay which was destroyed in 1635 by Roque Borges in the course of the pursuit of Dom Jeronimo. It was quickly rebuilt and continued to be used as a port for the west coast trade throughout the eighteenth century.

The Sakalava and the Bara settled on the west coast and were among the first to create kingdoms as opposed to tribal federations. At the height of their power they controlled one-third of the island but were unable to stand up to the English muskets and English-trained soldiers of the Imerina. Apart from the remarkable tradition of erotic funeral sculpture in wood, they seem to have left no historical monuments.

The Iharana founded a series of towns on the north-east coast of Madagascar of which Vohémar is the best known. They were Muslims but they retained an elaborate funeral ritual, utterly at variance with the principles of Islam. The excavations at Vohémar have produced Islamic glazed ware, porcelain, swords, glass beads and a curious three-footed pot carved in a soft stone which was placed at the feet of the corpse. According to the Portuguese writer Couto, Vohémar was founded by an Arab from Malindi, but the skeletons are a mixed, strongly Africanized type. The Antemoro of the south-east, who possess the magical books called Sorabe, written in Malagasy though in Arabic script, and other, originally Arab, elements in the population of the south-east are derived from the Iharana.

The date of these immigrations is unknown but it is possible that they may be as late as the thirteenth century, and the extension to the south-east as late as the fifteenth.

Apart from the Antalaot and the Iharana, the culture and political organization of the Malagasies remained primitive until the middle of the seventeenth century. The replacement of the clan by the kingdom was the result of the introduction of firearms by the Europeans in exchange for the cattle, rice and slaves which they took from the island. The trade, which had been largely conducted through the ports of the northwest, was extended to the east with the development by the French of the Mascarene Islands of Mauritius, Reunion and Rodriguez.

Organized European settlement on the island itself was confined to the south where the settlement at Fort Dauphin, started in 1643, was finally abandoned in 1674. The ruins of the fort can still be seen. However, in the last quarter of the eighteenth century the havens on the east coast, notably St. Marie and Antongil Bay, became the home of the pirates who settled on the coast, married the daughters of local chiefs, took part in local wars, and generally participated in the life of the country. The son of one of them, named Thomas White, was sent to England to be educated; came back, married the daughter of the Sakalava King of Bueni and founded a kingdom which lasted for three generations. The pirates have left little trace of themselves, except names cut in the rocks. They seem to have prided themselves on their literacy, as much as modern soldiers on leave and a certain type of tourist. So far as buried treasure is concerned, it is well to remember that before looking for a needle in a haystack one should establish that the needle exists. The pirates were lavish spenders, and they were always able to dispose of their gains to the honest traders who provided them with guns, rum and passages back to Europe or America. The more successful and intelligent of them resumed their normal life as soon as possible, but at a higher social and economic level than when they had left home.

The arrival of Captain Mathews and an English squadron on the coast in 1724 led to a hurried evacuation of St. Marie, and piracy ceased to be the lucrative game it had been in the past. Traders continued to come and deal with the Malagasy

22. Qibla of Mosque, Songo Mnara. Fourteenth or fifteenth century.

23(a) Fortress of S. Sebastião, Moçambique. Seventeenth century. Bastion of S. Gabriel.

  (b) Fortress of S. Sebastião, Moçambique, Chapel Nossa Senhora de Baluarte. Early sixteenth century.

chiefs through Europeans or creoles who lived on the coast. At the end of the eighteenth century the Hova Kingdom of Imerina was being formed and between 1810 and 1828 extended itself over two-thirds of the island.

On the mainland and on the inshore islands there were a number of Arab towns dependent on Kilwa, of which Moçambique was the most important, but even Moçambique is described as having only the mosque and the sheikh's house built of stone. The present township of Moçambique has nothing of the Arab about it. It is a small Portuguese seaport with a massive fortress at the seaward end commanding the entrance to the harbour. Actually, it never succeeded in preventing hostile ships entering the harbour, but the fortress was the strong point on which the whole Portuguese position on the Zambezi depended. During the eighteenth century it was the only European settlement on the east coast of Africa.

Moçambique was the first Arab-African town at which Vasco da Gama touched on his way to India. In 1507 it was chosen as the southern headquarters of the Portuguese and the principal port of call on the way to India. It was intended to be a place where ships could land their sick and dying and take on provisions for the last hop to India. Unfortunately the hospital arrangements were never adequate and the climate was so unhealthy that it was even recommended that ships should not touch at Moçambique, but go straight across to avoid further loss. Provisions were always difficult and at times were brought from as far as Pemba. There is no water on the island, and the town and fortress are dependent on cisterns, which causes great hardship if the rains are delayed.

The first buildings were a small fort, a hospital, a Dominican convent and three churches. Around them the merchant settlers built their mansions. All these buildings of the sixteenth century were destroyed by the Dutch in their two raids on the island in 1607 and 1608. The only structure of this period is a small square chapel dedicated to Nossa Senhora do Baluarte, Our Lady of the Bulwark, which stands on the promontory beyond the later fortress (Plate

o

23*b*). Around the roof is a frieze of Manoeline ornament, and over the door are the royal arms of Portugal with an armillary sphere, the badge adopted by Portugal in commemoration of her amazing achievements in navigation in the fifteenth century. Some of the gargoyles which take the water off the roof have the conventional medieval lion's heads; others are cannon barrels in stone. The same grim fancy is shown in the small windows which have the form of key-hole gunports. It was not for nothing that the chapel was named Our Lady of the Bulwark. The covered porch and the pulpit construction are not part of the original design and were added in the eighteenth century. There is something strange and haunting about this small, whitewashed chapel; it is as if the whole tragic history of the sea was wrapped up in this lonely little building, cut off from the world of the living by the great, grey walls of the fortress.

> Live those whom life shall cure, almost of memory,
> And leave us to endure our immortality.†

The present fortress, S. Sebastião, was commenced in 1558 (Plate 23*a* and Fig. 19). It covers an area of five acres and is the most impressive historical monument in East Africa. The first Captain to reside in the fortress was Nuno Velho Pereira (1583) but the work on the walls was still going on in 1595. The site had been chosen by João de Castro, the hero of the defence of Diu and one of the greatest of the Portuguese Viceroys of India, but building was not begun until ten years later for lack of an engineer. In the three attacks on the fort attempts were made to undermine the walls, which would have been impossible at Fort Jesus standing on its coral ridge.

The fortress occupies the south-east corner of the island and is surrounded on three sides by the sea. It is trapezoidal in plan with the longest face covering the harbour. It consists of a central court with raised bastions at the four corners: S. João, Nossa Senhora, and S. Antonio (now called S. Barbara) on the seaward side, and S. Gabriel towards the

† Kipling. *Collected Poems* (p. 392).

town. The curtain walls between the bastions are drawn back, forming a wide obtuse angle, a practice which was not approved by the Italian architects of the sixteenth century. Its adoption at Moçambique suggests that the plan is early sixteenth century, before the

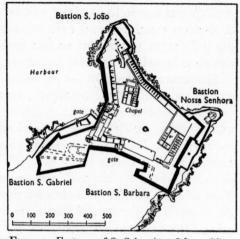

FIG. 19. *Fortress of S. Sebastiao, Moçambique*

Italian school had made its influence felt abroad. It had the same fashionable re-entrant angles on the vulnerable land-ward front as at Fort Jesus. One of these has survived at S. Barbara; the opposite angle at S. Gabriel was filled in when the bastion was reconstructed, perhaps at the beginning of the eighteenth century. The top of the wall of the re-entrant angle can be seen on the floor of the bastion.

There were originally three gates: the main gate on the landward side between S. Gabriel and S. Barbara, a secondary gate on the harbour side between S. João and S. Gabriel, and a postern gate in the middle of the sea wall leading to a couraça or breastwork which ran along the front of the fortress. When the couraça was destroyed by the sea, this was blocked and two gates made beside the two seaward bastions to pro-vide access to the new couraças in front of them. The old main gate was blocked at the time of the siege of 1607 and has only recently been re-opened. It is about five feet above the level of the ground outside and in front of it can be seen the support of the drawbridge, or rather one of the supports of the timber bridge by which access to the fort was provided. Inside the entrance were holes in the roof by which projectiles could be thrown at assailants who had forced the outer gate.

A ditch was dug in front of the wall between S. Gabriel and S. Barbara which has now been filled-in. It was intended to dig it from sea to sea, but no one could be found with the technical knowledge to make lock gates.

The secondary gate on the harbour side became the main gate in 1607 but the present façade, according to the inscription, was not erected until 1712. Above it are three blocked arches of an earlier façade. The change of gates was an improvement. The harbour gate can only be approached by a narrow track between the wall of the fort and the rocky shore. It would be impossible to mount siege batteries in front of it or to drive trenches for mining parties through the coral. The Portuguese had learnt the weakness of the other flank from their experiences during the sieges by the Dutch. Both gates were open to point blank fire from, in the first case, cannon on ships, and in the second, cannon landed on the island. At Fort Jesus the main gate is under the lee of S. Matias bastion and was always protected from the sea; later it was protected from the land by the elliptical bastion.

Inside the fortress are a number of buildings, including a chapel and cistern. From the records none of these constructions could have been completed before the late seventeenth century. Francisco de Mello e Castro, Captain in 1754, carried out many improvements in the Fort and many of these buildings may be his work. Until they can be investigated it is impossible to date them. The chapel was burnt down and subsequently used as a kitchen, but has now been restored.

The bastions of S. Sebastião, unlike those of Fort Jesus, have been changed in profile, particularly the two most important, S. Gabriel and S. Antonio, later known as S. Barbara. The present fortress has little resemblance to the fortress shown on the Texeira (c. 1610) and Rezende (c. 1636) plans, or the more reliable description of the Fort in the text of Rezende.

In the text the four bastions are said to be triangular; today it would be more correct to describe three as square and only S. Gabriel as triangular. More important perhaps than the choice of words is the statement repeated throughout the seventeenth century that work is in progress on S. Gabriel and S. Antonio, and the evidence of the tops of the walls of the earlier layout on the floor of the bastions. In the first half of the seventeenth century there are continual references to the reconstruction of S. Antonio, which was apparently not completed until the captaincy of Francisco de Lima (1652–56). However, the major modifications were carried out to S. Gabriel, considered the key to the fortress, which was greatly enlarged so that it finally stretched out towards the town like the big claw of a hermit crab. It is possible that the re-entrant angles, so popular in the late sixteenth-century fortresses, are an addition, later than Rezende and the work of Francisco de Lima. The re-entrant angle which survives in S. Antonio has a curious oval-shaped opening about ten feet from the ground, presumably for a cannon to cover the gate. Behind it are walls, possibly belonging to the original bastion before the reconstruction. Subsequently the re-entrant angle of S. Gabriel was filled in and the bastion enlarged. Finally it was enlarged again, with the curious hollow angle facing the approach from the town. This may be as late as the end of the eighteenth century.

The Chapel of Nossa Senhora has already been mentioned. Nearby, between the Bastion of Nossa Senhora and the seaward face of S. Antonio, is a stretch of flat ground bounded by a low wall, which was used as a place of execution and a cemetery.

The three great incidents in the history of the fortress and Moçambique are the two sieges by the Dutch, in 1607 and 1608, and an attack by an Omani fleet in 1670. On each occasion the Fort was defended with great gallantry by a ridiculously small and ill-equipped garrison.

On March 30, 1607 a Netherlands squadron, comprising three large ships and between one thousand and one thousand five hundred men, under Admiral Paulus van Caarden, was despatched to seize Moçambique. The town was occupied, guns were landed from the ships and batteries were mounted to bombard the Fort. The garrison consisted of sixty soldiers and about the same number of civilians; the few cannon were mostly unmounted and there were no trained gunners. The assault was directed against the main gate and the wall between S. Gabriel and S. Barbara. The walls were judged too strong to be breached. The assailants therefore dug trenches out from their field works towards the wall, so as to bring it down by mining. A wooden tower was built and pushed forward to within thirty paces of the wall. The defenders, under Captain Dom Estevão de Ataidé, fought back with muskets, powder pots and burning pitch. On April 29, when the trenches were only sixteen paces from the wall, the Captain carried out a successful counter-attack, which was enough to shake the resolution of the Dutch commander. On May 16, after burning the town and cutting down the palms, he ordered the soldiers to re-embark. The Fort was saved.

A year later the ordeal was repeated. A stronger expedition of nine large ships and one thousand eight hundred men under Vice-Admiral Pieter Verhoeven arrived on May 28, 1608. The town was taken and the attack on the fortress, with the digging of trenches and the pushing forward of batteries, followed the same pattern as the previous year. Part of the main wall was breached but the gap was filled with sand bags, and the defenders made a successful sortie, which showed there was no weakening in the spirit to resist. An attempt to drive a mine under the wall failed when fire-pots were hurled on the heads of the pioneers. On August 11, Verhoeven decided to break off the operations, and on August 18, the Netherlanders withdrew after burning the town and cutting down the remaining trees.

Before they withdrew there occurred one of those incidents, unimportant except to the unfortunate persons concerned, which provide the highlights of history. On August 15, four Dutch soldiers, tiring of life on the ships, deserted and were hauled up into the Fort with musket shots smacking the walls around them. The Dutch commander, rather like a communist government of today, instead of being delighted at having lost four unsatisfactory servants, took it as an injury and threatened to shoot thirty Portuguese prisoners he had taken unless they were returned. Dom Estevão had shown that he could not be intimidated. He now showed that he could not be blackmailed. He refused to surrender the fugitives and six of the thirty prisoners were actually shot in front of the Fort. It would be nice to record that the four Dutch fugitives showed themselves worth the sacrifice that had been made for them. Not a bit of it. On the contrary they turned out to be idle good-for-nothings and the Portuguese were soon heartily sick of them.

Dom Estevão should have died then or gone away with his glory. Instead he was appointed Governor of the Conquest of the Mines in addition to Captain of Moçambique. After three years of extortion and incompetence on the Zambezi, he was dismissed and recalled to appear before a court of enquiry. But he had already received a summons to a higher court and on September 8, 1613 the hero of S. Sebastião died, a broken pauper in the Jesuit College of S. Paul at Moçambique.

In 1670 a large fleet of eighteen ships with Arabs from Muscat sacked and burnt the town and are said to have attacked the Fort. According to a story reported by Burton they did succeed in undermining the walls, but the defenders exploded a counter mine which induced the Arabs to withdraw. The Captain and most of the soldiers were away on the Zambezi but the Fort was bravely defended by the *alcaide-mor* or administrative officer, Gasper de Sousa de Laçerda, and a handful of soldiers and civilians.

This was the last military engagement in which the Fort featured. In 1756 it ceased to be the residence of the Captain, who moved to a house in the town and later to the Jesuit College. The Captain's house became the residence of the next ranking military officer. The soldiers continued to live in the Fort and during the last fifty years it was used also as a jail. Now there is only a small unit quartered in the Fort and a beginning has been made in its conversion into an historical monument and museum.

The old town was burnt during the three sieges of the seventeenth century; the buildings seen today date largely from the eighteenth century. The oldest is the Governor's Palace, once the Jesuit College of S. Paulo, which was built in the first half of the seventeenth century. With the suppression of the Jesuit Order by the Marquis de Pombal, it became in 1763 the residence of the Captain-General, at last independent of the Viceroy of Goa. The steps in front of the Palace were added at this time and other alterations to make it more convenient for an official residence. The chapel has retained much of its seventeenth-century character and the High Altar and Pulpit are fine examples of Portuguese-Indian stonework. On the right wall is the plaque in honour of Dom Estevão which was put up by the Jesuit Fathers whom he had strongly supported in the days of his authority and who had looked after him in his days of disgrace.

The old cathedral has disappeared, and the present cathedral is the church of the Misericordia which was probably built in the later seventeenth century. The façade is dated 1700 but the church was reconstructed in 1770. The Misericordia was a charitable institution which existed in all towns in Portugal and in the colonies, to which people with a social conscience, and those who hadn't but felt they ought to appear to have, liked to belong. It looked after the sick, managed their estates when they died, and cared for their orphans, legitimate or otherwise. It performed many of the functions which the welfare state now performs without thanks and without honour, more efficiently but at great expense to the community. The Misericordia was extinguished in 1915, in accordance with the republican policy of separating church and state. The church had been used since 1883 as the Parish Church after the collapse of the cathedral.

The other old church, Nossa Senhora de Saude, was founded by the Capuchins in 1633 but in 1646 passed into the hands of the Brothers of S. João de Deus. It was restored in 1801 and is now in the care of the Brotherhood of S. Vincente de Paul.

There are some fine old-world houses built by merchants

216

and landowners at various periods of prosperity, mostly at the end of the nineteenth century.

Between the island and the mainland is the small island fort S. Lourenço, built at the end of the seventeenth century to guard the southern passage which was navigable for small boats of Arab type. It is a well-built fortress, triangular in shape, but seems never to have had an opportunity to show its quality.

On the mainland to the north, at Cabeceira, is the fine eighteenth-century church of Nossa Senhora de Remedios, and the remains of the late eighteenth-century fort of Mossuril.

Off Cape Delgado to the north, the boundary between the territories of the captains of Moçambique and Malindi, are the Kerimba Islands. The principal town, presumably the present centre of Ibo, was sacked by the Portuguese under Pedro de Castro in 1522, at the instigation of the sultans of Zanzibar and Pemba. They said the islands had been accustomed to pay tribute to them but had now become subject to the Sultan of Mombasa. The Portuguese ignored the claims of all three rulers and took the islands for themselves. The islands were leased to Portugal and the inhabitants were obliged to pay twenty-one per cent of their crops and a tithe to the church—rather the same proportion of their earnings as they would have to pay to the government if they were living in England today. They took it with similar resignation, and the good relations between the settlers and subjects were a matter of comment. One's doubts as to the good relations are to some extent relieved by the fact that at the beginning of the siege of Fort Jesus in 1696, an emissary sent to the island for help, reported that there were thirty-seven Portuguese capable of bearing arms but only six or seven possessed weapons. The Portuguese landlord lived in a fort and there were two churches for his tenants.

The present triangular fort was built in 1791 to protect the island against Sakalava raids from Madagascar. Owen mentioned an expedition of sixty-eight canoes which set out from Bembatooka in 1816 and ended in complete disaster.

Coir rope, rice and cattle were the principal products of

the islands, which were a valuable source of supply for Moçambique.

Between Moçambique and Sofala were Quilimane and Angoche, old Arab settlements but no more developed than Moçambique. Their inhabitants during the sixteenth and seventeenth centuries were able to run the Portuguese blockade and compete successfully in the gold trade. Both enjoyed considerable prosperity from the boom in the slave trade that marked the later eighteenth and early nineteenth centuries. No old buildings have survived.

The fortress of Sofala, commenced in 1505, has disappeared completely but in the museum at Lourenço Marques are some of the arches and carved stone shields sent from Portugal. There is no stone at Sofala and the repeated orders optimistically sent from Lisbon for the construction of a fortress were particularly difficult to carry out. In any case Quiliman was a better outlet for the trade of the Zambezi. Sofala has a great name in the history of commerce but there was never a town, even in the modest sense of the word accepted in East Africa. At the time of the arrival of the Portuguese there were two small settlements and the fortress was constructed between the one at the mouth of the river and the other half a league from the bar. The Portuguese settlement was most flourishing at the beginning of the seventeenth century, but fifty years later was in decline.

South of Sofala there were intermittent Portuguese posts in Delagoa Bay; it was not until the end of the eighteenth century, after two abortive attempts by Dutch and Austrians to build forts and start trading establishments, that the Portuguese built the present Red Fort which was the nucleus of Lourenço Marques. Lourenço Marques in its early days was a punishment station, and a lurid account of the captains of the early nineteenth century is given by Owen. Succession by assassination was irregular even in the earliest days of colonial administration. The Red Fort had been restored but it is the original building. It is now used as a museum where, in addition to the stones from Sofala, there is a fine collection of nineteenth-century arms which are looked after with admirable care.

Bibliography

It would be inappropriate to cumber a popular book with footnotes, but for readers who wish to check my statements or to go further into the subject I give below a select bibliography, which should provide the necessary information or the means to it, or add greater confusion. The history of man in East Africa is still in its infancy.

AXELSON, E. *South-East Afrika 1488–1530.* 1940.
    South-East Afrika 1600–1700. 1960.
COUPLAND, R. *East Africa and its Invaders.* 1938.
    The Exploitation of East Africa, 1856–90. 1939.
DUYVENDAK, J. J. L. *China's Discovery of Africa.* 1949.
FREEMAN-GRENVILLE, G. S. P. *The East African Coast (Select Documents from the First to the Earlier Nineteenth Century).* 1962.
GROTTANELLI, V. L. *Pescatori del Oceano Indiano.* 1955.
GUILLAIN, M. *Documents sur l'histoire, la geographie et le commerce de l'Afrique oriental.* 1856–58.
HARDINGE, SIR ARTHUR *A Diplomatist in the East.* 1939.
HILL, M. *Permanent Way, Vol. II.* 1958.
INGHAM, K. *History of East Africa.* 1962.
KRAPF, J. L. *Travels, Researches and Missionary Labours during an eighteen years' residence in East Africa.* 1860.
MURDOCH, G. P. *Africa. Its Peoples and their Culture History.* 1960.
OWEN, W. F. W. *Narrative of voyages to explore the shores of Africa, Arabia and Madagascar.* 1833.
PRINS, A. H. J. *The Swahili-Speaking Peoples of Zanzibar and the East African Coast.* 1961.
SCHOFF, W. H. *The Periplus of the Erythrean Sea,* 1912.
STRANDES, J. *The Portuguese Period in East Africa.* 1961. (translation with notes of *Die Portugiesenzeit von Deutsch und Englisch Ostafrika.* 1899.
Tanganyika Notes and Records 1936—

Somalia

CERULLI, E. *Somalia.* 1957.
CURLE, A. T. *Ruined Towns of Somaliland.* Antiquity, 1937.

Kenya

BOXER, C. R. AND CARLOS DE AZEVEDO. *Fort Jesus & the Portuguese in Mombasa.* 1960.
GRAY, SIR JOHN. *The British in Mombasa, 1824–26.* 1957.
HICHENS, W. *Khabar al-Lamu.* Bantu Studies xii. 1938.
HINAWY, SIR MBARAK BIN ALI. *al-Akida and Fort Jesus, Mombasa.* 1950.
KIRKMAN, J. S. *Excavations at Kilepwa.* Ant. J. xxxii. 1952.
   The Arab City of Gedi. Excavations at the Great Mosque. Architecture and Finds. 1952.
   Historical Archaeology in Kenya, 1948–56. Ant. J. xxxvii. 1957.
   Kinuni. An Arab Manor on the Coast of East Africa. J. Roy. Asiatic Soc. 1957.
   The Great Pillars of Malindi and Mambrui. Oriental Art. 1958.
   Takwa. The Mosque of the Pillar. Ars Orientalis II, 1957.
   Mnarani of Kilifi. Ars Orientalis III. 1959.
   Fort Jesus Guide. 1960.
   Gedi—The Palace. 1963.
PRINS, A. H. J. *The Coastal Tribes of the North-East Bantu.* 1952.
STIGAND, C. H. *The Land of Zinj.* 1913.
WERNER, A. *A Swahili History of Pate.* J. A. Soc. xiv. 1915.

Zanzibar

BUCHANAN, L. A. C. *Ancient Monuments of Pemba.* 1937.
GRAY, SIR JOHN *History of Zanzibar to 1856.* 1962.
PEARCE, F. B. *Zanzibar.* 1920.

Tanganyika

Annual Reports Department of Antiquities 1957—
FREEMAN-GRENVILLE, G. S. P. *Mediaeval History of Tanganyika.* 1962.

Moçambique

LOBATO, A. *A Ilha de Moçambique.* 1945.

Madagascar

DESCHAMPS, H. *Histoire de Madagascar*. 1961.

The best bibliographies are to be found in Prins, Axelson and the English edition of Strandes. Many of the works cited are in journals which are extremely difficult to find even in large libraries. An *Oxford History of East Africa* and a new edition of the *Periplus of the Erythrean Sea* by Dr. G. Mathew are in preparation. For coins there are two articles by J. Walker in the Numismatic Chronicle 1936 and 1939, and Freeman-Grenville's more recent articles in *Numismatic Chronicle* 1957 and in *Journal of African History I.* 1. 1960. For modern coins see W. H. Valentine, *Modern Copper Coins of the Muhammadan States*, 1911.

Index

223